LIFE IS NOT ALL GOOD… IT'S ALL GOD

FRANK LUKE

All Scripture quotes are taken from the King James, New King James and English Standard Versions of the Holy Bible

DEDICATION

This book is dedicated to My Lord and Savior Jesus Christ. In You I live, breathe, move and have my being.

To my mother, Loretta Luke. You introduced me to Jesus Christ at a very young age and for that I will forever be grateful. I will forever honor you for the sacrifices you made and the strength you exemplified so that I would have an opportunity to become the man I am today. I am honored to call you my mother.

To my three wonderful kids, Aric Flemming Jr., Nia and Zion Luke. Your existence is my motivation to be the best I can be in every aspect of my life. You are a blessing for the Most High God, and I cherish every moment He's given me to be your father and friend. I pray that you always hold on to His un-changing hand.

To the mother of my kids, DeJuan Luke. I will always respect you for entrusting me with our son Aric and for sacrificially blessing me with our youngest two children, Nia and Zion. A great deal of the knowledge, strength, and wisdom I have acquired over the years, has come from the journey we shared together. For that I am thankful.

To my big sister, Michelle Bates. We don't talk much, but when we do its refreshing to know the love is always there. I love you and I thank God that you are my sister.

To my big brother Stanley Bates. Although you're not here with me in body, I'm always inspired by the love and protection I feel from your spirit. My ministry is inspired by you. My drive to be great in God's kingdom is inspired by the desire you had to be great in His kingdom. I will always love you. Thank you for watching over me.

PRAISE FOR LIFE IS NOT ALL GOOD…IT'S ALL GOD

In a world where transparency and authenticity means very little, Frank Luke delivers a powerfully honest book about faith, survival and redemption. For those of us who are fighting to overcome odds, outlive our past, and find hope for our future, this book is a must-read. Every page of this amazing read is screaming, "Don't stop living – your pain will soon pass." The author bears his soul, shares his heart and tells us a story of resilience that speaks to the core of our common human experiences. This is the book to have when you need to hear God telling you that, "All things work together for your good."
~ Pastor Marlin D. Harris, New Life Church

I have known Frank Luke for many years now and I have seen him grow in the grace of God. He is a man of wisdom and godly integrity. There is no doubt in my mind "Life is not all good… It's all God" will be a blessing to all that read it.
~R&B Artist Keith Sweat

TABLE OF CONTENTS

ACKNOWLEDGMENTS

I want to start by acknowledging my pastor, father in the ministry, and friend, Pastor Marlin Harris. I can never repay you for all the knowledge and wisdom you have poured into my family and me over the many years. You saw something great in me, long before I saw it in myself. Thank you for believing in me and blessing me to go out and speak the Word of truth, in and out of season.

To my clients, there are too many to name. I thank you all for the many years you have allowed me to serve you as your barber and stylist. I would not be the man I am today if it wasn't for the fellowship we've had for countless years. You have been more than clients, you have been my friends.

A great big thank you to those I call "The Crew": Will and Tanya Wilson, Cori and Twanna Brock, Steve and Justina Jenkins, and Erika Foxworth. When I was at one of the lowest points in my life, it was your prayers and friendship that held me up. I cease not to mention you in my prayers.

A special thanks to Greg and Cassandra Booth, Rev. Charles and Ann Oggs, and George and Celena Matlock. Thank you for always being there and helping me figure out the details of life. You have been the best big brothers and sisters in Christ a man could ask for.

Thank you Kent and Annette Osby for your many years of support.

I dare not forget to mention my cousin Tammy Rogers. You stepped in like a big sister and made sure I was well in mind and spirit.

To my angel in disguise, Vivian Fisher, you may not fully understand how blessing me with the website design and book changed my paradigm of faith. Your gift to me showed me that God wasn't just answering my prayers, but He was ushering me into something beyond my understanding. Thank you for inspiring me to go the next level.

Last but not least, I must thank the men's ministry, Men Leading from Their Knees (MLFTK) for all of your prayers and support.

And to everyone who has been a part of this journey, thank you.

FRANK LUKE

CHAPTER 1
INTRODUCTION

From the moment a child is conceived in his mother's womb until the day he departs from this world, there is very little that can be done to avoid the many obstacles and challenges that are destined to be a part of life. Childbearing is one of the greatest phenomenon in life, if not the greatest. The overall process of birth is much like the process of living. Once the seed of the man fertilizes the egg of a female, the maturing process begins. Much like a fertilized egg has to go through a series of transforming developments before it becomes a child ready to be born, such is life. There are transforming challenges we must endure before we reach the stage of birthing our dreams and walking in our God-ordained purpose. The metamorphic experience that takes place between mother and fetus is absolutely astonishing. From fertilized egg to embryo, the baby along with its mother begins a journey. Cells begin to split and separate. Time goes on, and after much splitting and separating, organs form, body parts form and baby starts to take shape. During this beautiful process, this once microscopic egg now has the form of an actual human being.

While life is being shaped in the mother's womb, her life is being reshaped in the womb of this world. Mother's body takes on the form of the incredible miracle growing inside of her. Her organs are forced to shift for the comfort of her internal passenger. Her emotions at times are imbalanced, her food cravings are beyond her control, many of her habits are forced to change. It is definitely a new experience for both mother and child.

I had the privilege of being a part of this experience when my wife carried and delivered our daughter and son. I was there to wait on her hand and foot and I was by her bedside encouraging her through both deliveries: two of the most beautiful experiences I've been a part of in life. Seeing that process first hand reminded me of life and its challenges.

My wife would have contractions that at times seemed unbearable. I swear if she had squeezed my hand any harder I would have thought I was having contractions. Every time she would have a contraction the doctor would tell her to push. Though the contractions were very painful (for both of us), the pain was a sign of purpose. When she felt pain she knew it was time to push. No painful moment was wasted, every time she felt pain it was an opportunity to push the baby closer to his or her purpose. In that moment, the experience is just as traumatic for the child. For months the child has been living without a care in the world. Periodically, through a sonogram we could see the baby laughing and playing. Occasionally, we could catch them stretching and adjusting to obtain the optimal position of comfort, all at the expense of my wife's discomfort. Every time the doctor instructed my wife to push, the baby was being forced down a narrow canal, against its will all in an effort to get to the next level. This mirrors life.

There will be seasons in our lives that are peaceful and stress free. However, we will come into seasons where we are split and separated. It may come from our actions and poor decisions or through no fault of our own. There will be times in our lives where we are seemingly being stretched to the point of breaking. Life can throw so many unexpected challenges at us that even our loved ones will feel our burdens.

Be assured, as long as you live, if you have not had to overcome any challenges in life, you will. Hardship is inevitable. Although this is a true statement, trust God. He has a plan and a purpose for every obstacle in your life. There is no challenge we face in life that Jesus has not already overcome. The Bible encourages us that He was tempted in all points as we and yet without sin (*Hebrews 4:15*). The Bible also assures us that He was wounded for our transgressions, our peace was upon Him and by His stripes we are healed (*Isaiah 53:5*). Despite the difficult times you may face, you must keep your head up and your heart open to the will of God.

Life can truly catch you off guard. Some things are just inexplicable. Some people are born into hardship and some people acquire it throughout the course of life. A child can be born with Down syndrome, Tourette's syndrome, Cancer, HIV or any other major disability. That child is considered to be born with a handicap. Encyclopedia.com defines a handicap is a condition that markedly restricts a person's ability to function physically, mentally, or socially.

Essentially, based on the definition, someone is born with a mark that will define how well or how poorly he functions in life. His handicap has defined the magnitude of his contribution to life. How productive he can be in the work force will always be a question. How competitive he can be in the athletic world will always be in doubt. These are challenges that he faces that had absolutely nothing to do with him. He was born into this.

Maybe you were not born with a debilitating illness that hinders your ability to physically or mentally perform, but being born into a broken home, a poverty stricken community, or an environment that is full of violence and instability can very well impede on your progress and make success appear to be more difficult than not.

We all have various stories to share. You may find it hard to relate to some of the previous scenarios because your formative years were full of fun, liberty and promise. Perhaps it wasn't until later in life, things took a drastic turn; that dream marriage suddenly ended in divorce, sudden death of a loved one, financial crisis, loss of job, home, or car. You name it, anything can happen at any time that could disrupt your mental, social, and physical ability to perform in a manner to which you're accustomed. I assure you if you haven't had to overcome any challenges in life that have made you feel like life just isn't fair, just keep living, you will.

Life is indicative to the seasons; they are constantly changing just like our circumstances. Some changes are healthy, some changes are seemingly unhealthy, but all change can be profitable with the proper perspective. Despite the changes life throws you, there is one thing about life that is constant and never changes. That's God. God is just as much a part of this life as you and I are. God is available when we are at our worst and when we are at our best.

Have you ever asked yourself these questions?
Why me?
When am I going to…?
What happened?

There are some questions that have absolute answers, and there are some questions that have absolutely no reasonable answer to man. Why a man would kill his entire family and then take his own life because the stock market crashed, we will never understand. Why are some children born with debilitating illnesses from two perceivably healthy parents? Science may never be able to provide an answer. There are some things that happen in life that only God has a reasonable answer for. He reserves the right to the why, when, and what and how He will reveal them to you. Despite all of the questions you may have there is one answer that remains true; God is in control and He has your best interest at heart!

As you prepare to take this journey through the pages of this book, many of the biblical applications and real life stories that are reflected will enhance your faith and wisdom, so that you may embrace your journey with much fervency. We will look at the life of Joseph and how he was *favored* by his father, *fell* into captivity by the hands of his brothers, and how he was *fortunate* in rising to be second in command by the glory of God. We will reflect on the words of David, the man the Bible addresses as a man after God's own heart. And we will explore pages of my real life story, how my paradigm was formed as a child. How I became a well-established "Celebrity Barber" at the age of nineteen, traveled the world, met and fellowshipped with many celebrities, and most of all, when I received a phone call to service the world's greatest: Muhammad Ali. I will share some of the challenges I have had to endure in life that brought me closer to God. I was diagnosed with Tourette's syndrome, lost my brother tragically to police violence and lastly, how I failed to save a marriage I thought would last forever. All of these things would have truly broken me if it wasn't for the grace of God. They developed me into the man God has anointed me to be today. Reflections such as these along with many other inspiring verses will prayerfully inspire you to look at your situation a little deeper, embrace the bigger picture and change your perspective on life. Know that God will not put more on you than you can bear and everything you go through has a purpose. Your universal and personal purpose is far greater than your temporary pain.

Life is not all good but it's certainly all God!

FRANK LUKE

CHAPTER 2
MIRACLES DO HAPPEN

I grew up doing many of the things normal boys do when they are adolescents. Climbing trees, playing football, riding bikes, sticking my hand in fire occasionally, to see if it was as hot as it looked. Normal stuff, right? Maybe not the fire part, but for the most part I was a basic, All-American little boy. I was rough, active and gave my mother a run for her money. I had no idea my life would be impacted in a major way.

I never considered myself a bad kid but I was very active and I was easily distracted. In my early years at school, my inability to stay focused kept me off task and occasionally in trouble for being a disruption to the class. I tried very hard to stay focused and when I would get in trouble, my teachers would tell my mom that I tried very hard to be a good kid. My mother was a loving woman but she was no stranger to firm correction. Let's just say, the verse that says "spare the rod, spoil the child" was well interpreted in my home. Needless to say, I was very thankful anytime my teachers would soften that dreaded phone call home to my mother.

As school years would come and go, the same stories would travel with me throughout every year. During study time, I would always get in trouble for not staying on task or being a distraction to someone else. When that dreadful phone call would come to my mom to have a conference concerning my behavior, they would all say the same thing, "He is such a good kid, but he cannot stay focused." Due to an increase in excessive distracting behavior, we soon found out that my behavior had a root cause beyond my control. Back in my day, most kids that were easily distracted and challenged with staying focused just as I was. If diagnosed with an issue, they were generally diagnosed with Attention Deficit Disorder (ADD). I remember a couple of kids in my class were diagnosed with this illness. I do not know what medication they were on, but I do know the medication would slow them down dramatically. They became almost zombie-like. When it was suggested this was possibly my problem and medication was recommended, my mother was not buying it. Neither was I. I was a child, but I could see that my behavior was not as extreme as the kids that were diagnosed with ADD. However, there was something wrong.

I do not remember the exact day or time that my mother made me aware that my behavior was strange. I remember very vividly standing in her bedroom and she asked me what I was doing. I replied in a baffled manner that I was not doing anything. To my knowledge I was just standing there. She asked me, "Why do you keep doing that?" I was very confused. Clearly my mother was seeing something I didn't see because I was not doing anything other standing there, talking and listening. Then I noticed she began to stare at me as if there was something going on with me or around me, that was just as clear to her as me standing there. And then I did it again, and again, and again. Whatever I was doing it became apparent to me that my body was reacting in a manner that was almost instinctive and systematic. I saw the shock on my mother's face, it was almost like she knew something was wrong but she was in somewhat of a disbelief that I was not aware of what I was doing. Incredulously, my mother asked me if I realized that my eyes were rolling back in my head, my head would jerk, and that I was making a snorting noise all at the same time. The more attention she brought to it the worse it would become. In times past, I could faintly remember my body reacting in an abnormal way, but I did not think it was that abnormal.

It would not be long before this thing that was once subtle and unassuming would become a dominant force to be reckoned with in my life. Once it was brought to my attention, it seemed that I was having these ticks a lot more regular. Every day on the hour I was having these ticks and the more I tried to stop and resist the urge my body was having to react in this manner, it felt like they became worse. It had really gotten out of hand. If I focused on who was watching me or looking at me strangely, it made the ticks almost unbearable. My ability to go to school and focus had become almost impossible and I was really battling with not being so self-conscious and insecure. It was extremely stressful. I could deal with not being the fastest amongst my peers or even the strongest. I was fairly cool and athletic and I had an older brother who paved a path for me, so popularity was not a concern of mine. But for a ten-year-old kid, this unforeseen issue that at that time had no proper diagnosis was really challenging how I perceived myself. This was also becoming very stressful for my mother. My mother was a single parent raising three kids on her own, and I was the youngest. She worked nights to provide food, shelter and clothes for us. I am sure that was challenging in and of itself. Added to that, she had this unforeseen issue with her youngest son that no one could seem to understand.

I had gone to all sorts of specialists; I went to an ophthalmology specialist, neurological specialist, and any other medical specialist that may have had some idea of what was going on. Nothing had worked. I remember one doctor putting me on medication that was primarily for people who were having seizures and for a brief time it seemed to work. When it stopped working with the recommended dosage, the doctor instructed my mother to increase the dosage by a whole pill instead of half. I cannot personally recall what actions followed the increase in dosage, but according to my mother, she had to rush me to the emergency room because the dosage that the doctor recommended put me in a delusional state. I had borderline overdosed.

My mother and I were in the fight of our lives. There were so many times I simply wanted to go to sleep and not wake up. Throughout the day I continued having these ticks nonstop and no one could properly diagnose what was going on. Sleep and high activity seemed to be the only real resolve for them. I was still an active boy, so sleep in the middle of the day was stressful. After all, what ten-year-old wants to take a nap?

My mother was desperate to find out what was going on with me and so was I. It was one thing to have these embarrassing ticks, but what was more alarming is that no would could diagnose the root of the problem. Throughout this whole ordeal my mother never stopped praying and believing God for a breakthrough. I remember my mother praying with spiritual leaders and having them pray for me. One day in particular, my mother picked me up from school and took me directly to a friend of hers who was a pastor known for doing spiritual warfare. My mother has always instilled in me a resiliency and determination. She never gave up on anything she believed in and surely she was not about to give up on her baby boy.

I remember these women of God surrounded me and they went to war. I remember them praying for my healing and God's protection over my life. To be honest, this experience was a little bit spooky for me. I believed in God, but at the age of ten, I did not fully understand these women putting their hands all over my head, back, and chest, telling this person named Satan that he could not have me. I did not fully understand their choice of words.

I had no clue Satan was after me. I did not know what after me meant. All in all, the belief I had in God overwhelmed the misunderstanding I had of Satan and I believed if Satan was *after* me; my mother, the pastor, and God were all after him.

We left there weeping with tears of joy, anticipating a breakthrough. Months passed and the symptoms remained but my mother never gave up hope. One night, she took me to the local hospital emergency room and demanded that they look at me again. She insisted that someone figure out what was wrong with me. It just so happened that a team of specialists from Emory Hospital were coming in later that morning and the staff doctor recommended we return later. Something in my mother's spirit insisted that we wait. We slept in the waiting chairs in the lobby until they arrived. I will never forget this day.

The doctors from Emory had finally arrived. They took me into a room, and they proceeded to ask all of the generic questions that were asked a million times before. After asking the necessary questions to gain an understanding of my circumstances, they all took a minute and just stared at me. It was an extremely awkward moment for me and I began to lose hope. They were going to be just like all the other doctors with no answers and no help for me. After staring at me seemingly for an eternity, the lead physician, Dr. Nicolas Krawiecki asked the other physicians a question. With a smirk on his face and an assurance in his eyes, he asked the other doctors if they knew what was wrong with me. Clueless and dumbfounded they all answered no. Without hesitation and with much confidence he announced, "This young man has Tourette's syndrome."

All of their eyes lit up in shock and disbelief. At the time, Tourette's syndrome was not a popular illness and my symptoms were not common. Although it was familiar in the Caucasian communities, it wasn't a familiar illness in the African American community. Tourette's syndrome is an inherited neuropsychiatric disorder with onset in childhood, characterized by multiple physical or motor ticks and at least one vocal or phonic tick. This explained why I did not recognize my symptoms early on until they were brought to my attention. My earlier motor ticks were very subtle; we would later learn what those earlier signs were.

Dr. Krawiecki brought my mother into the room, sat her down and told her his diagnosis. He explained to her all the symptoms that came with this illness and informed her she would feel very guilty for some of the things she had chastised me for as kid that I had no control over. He told her there was no cure but he recommended a medication for high blood pressure called Clonidine (Cat après) and he felt that would suppress the symptoms. That was my all mother needed to hear. It was a tremendous relief to finally know what was going on but my mother was not done. An incurable illness for her son was not an option.

The medication seemed to work for a while but my mom never accepted I would be on medication for the rest of my life. She continued to believe I would be healed. My symptoms remained for about another year or so before we saw a difference. I was taking half of a pill every night and it seemingly calmed my symptoms. My mother being the mother she is, decided to take a risk. She started restricting me from taking the medication for a period of time, I guess to see if God was working or maybe she just did not like the fact I was constantly taking medication in an effort to manage everyday life.

Now that we knew what we were dealing with, the love, understanding, and support we received from family, friends, and school staff was overwhelming. My teachers fell in love with me all over again. Since my teachers realized I was not being a tyrant the many times I disrupted the class, I guess they were feeling a little guilty for sending me to the office or calling my mom so much. I remember my fifth grade English teacher was so apologetic when she found out I had an illness. She told my mother she thought the times my eyes would roll back that I was rolling my eyes on purpose as a form of disrespect. Surprisingly, my peers embraced me even more. I never had any problems with my peers before, but you know how mean kids can be. I thought surely they would take advantage of an opportunity to make fun of my disability. I can't honestly say I embraced the notion that I could possibly be taking medication for the rest of my life. But, once I had knowledge of my illness I was able to manage my stress level much better by staying active, occasionally taking my meds, and yes, sleeping. Living with my dysfunction was much easier.

Little did I know, my mother was behind the scenes watching and praying... watching and praying... watching and praying according to Mark 13:33. Having such a great anticipation that I would one day be totally healed, every time my symptoms would slow down I would immediately claim my healing. At times, I would stop taking my medication believing I was healed and to my despair the symptoms would return and I would be crushed. My mother never stopped believing.

At some point, the medication was not working as effectively as we wanted and neither I nor my mother were open to increase the dosage. When I ran out of the medication, my mother did not refill it and she encouraged me to believe I was healed, so I did. I was sick of having tics. I was sick of going to the doctor and I was sick of taking medication. I felt like God was my last and only hope.

One day my mother said to me, "Frank, do you realize you haven't had any ticks in a while and you haven't been on your medication?" With a baffled expression, I stood there for a second just to allow her observation to register. She was correct. I wasn't having any ticks! At that moment with a huge smile on her face, she immediately picked up the phone and started calling any and everyone who would listen to share with them that I was healed. You would think she would have shared this pertinent information with me first. I was the recipient of this miracle and I didn't have a clue I was healed I just knew I my ticks weren't active at that time. That's how Mrs. Luke operates. I guess she figured since I didn't recognize I was healed it didn't make sense trying to share that with me. She needed to communicate and rejoice with someone who could relate to the struggle. Besides, I was a kid. Even though in times past I would rejoice with every moment that I had previously believed I was healed because my symptoms were suppressed, by that time I was just tired and glad it was over. It didn't matter much to me. I was just glad I wasn't having anymore ticks and I wasn't making those embarrassing snorkeling noises. I knew something big had transpired and I knew the God I believed in was the cause of it. I didn't fully grasp the significance of my healing. By the time I reached high school and more studies had been done concerning Tourette's Syndrome, I would learn more about the illness and I would see the challenges that thousands of young people and their parents were having with this illness. It was then I would think to myself, Wow! God delivered me from that!

Here I am thirty plus years later, removed from all signs and symptoms of Tourette's syndrome. I do not remember the specific day or time it happened. I now realize God was not my last and only hope. He is my first and only hope. Allow me to share with you what I mean. It was only a short time after the prayer session with my mother's friend that my mother was led, out of desperation, to take me to that hospital emergency room in the early hours of the morning. It just so happened to be the day the specialist from a neighboring hospital would be arriving. It just so happened out of the five specialists that had no clue to what was going on with me, there was one who did. I know God is a Healer, and He is a Miracle Worker. My mother's impulsive decision to take me to the hospital in the early hours of the morning when the one doctor that knew what was going on with me would be there that morning was no accident. It was a divine move of God. I encourage you to believe in Him. What the world deems as impossible, in God, is possible because there is nothing impossible for God.

Now unto Him who is able to do exceedingly abundantly above all that we ask or think, according to the power that works in us,
Ephesians 3:20 NKJV

CHAPTER 3
UNEXPECTED BLESSINGS

There are so many books, life coaches and professionals that can instruct you on how to obtain wealth, how to get the biggest bang for your buck. Even the internet has a profusion of information at your disposal to advise and guide you in any direction of professional choice. If you have the desire to be an actor, a producer, a rapper, a dog trainer or an entrepreneur of any sort, there is so much information to help you in obtaining your desired success. There is almost no excuse for failure. It is imperative to exercise all of the avenues possible to aid in an individual's level of success. However, I have come to learn that no book, counselor, life coach, established businessman or women can set you up for success better than God himself.

There are not many kids at the ripe old age of thirteen that can honestly say they know exactly what they want to do as it relates to their career goals when they grow up.

Not to say that there aren't any, but most kids at that age are just coming into their own identity, they are not trying to figure out what career path they want to travel. If you are a young person reading this and you are one of the few who knows what you want in life at a very early age, you're on your way to big things. But most kids are only concerned with the latest and greatest video game or, the hottest shoes on the market. If you have a kid who at an early age is crunching numbers, reading as a hobby, or doing volunteer work at a local veterinarian hospital or elderly patient home, that's an anomaly. You have a prodigy on your hands.

I was one of the unusual kids. I realized around the age of twelve that I had a natural talent to cut hair and give people their desired style. I realized I had this ability when I was in the barbershop one day and I could feel and comprehend what the barber was doing as he cut my hair. As I perused the room, I was soaking in everything the other barbers were doing as if I were sitting at their feet taking one on one lessons. I was so anxious to get home and pull out the clippers. My mother was also naturally gifted to style women's hair, so we always had clippers, flat irons and hair products somewhere in the house. When I arrived home, I immediately jumped into trimming over what my barber had done and it was a euphoric moment. I knew immediately this was what I was destined to do. I was so energized by how natural it was for me to understand the concept of fading and trimming the hair with certain angles to obtain desired looks. I sought after every opportunity I could to absorb more information and broaden my knowledge on the craft. I would go to sweep up the barbershop or just sit around watching my barber and others operate in their craft. It wouldn't be many years after, I would become a well-recognized neighborhood barber myself.

All day, every day, I thought about cutting hair. It would not be long before a door opened that would inspire me on another level. My cousin told her hairstylist about me and asked if she would be willing to give me a shot in her newly opened salon. I met with the hairstylist in her salon in Downtown Atlanta. I was around sixteen-years-old at this time and it was a long shot trying to get in a salon with an opportunity to cut hair. Everyone else wanted to keep me as clean up kid. I interviewed with the owner of the salon and based on the recommendation from my cousin she would give me an undeserved opportunity. I was not of age nor did I have any certification to support me working in a salon as a barber.

My first day reporting to work was a humbling experience. I had the confidence of a full-grown lion in my community, being heralded as the best barber in the neighborhood. The moment I walked into this lion's den AKA the hair salon surrounded by other professional barbers and stylist, needless to say, I was very intimidated. The stylists had enough equipment for themselves and five other people. All I had was a couple pair of clippers, a neck duster, some isopropyl alcohol and a covering cape. The owner asked me if I was ready and at that moment I felt like I was on trial. I could not disappoint my cousin nor could I allow my intimidation to cause me to embarrass myself.

When the owner sent a client to me, I remember I was so nervous but I continued to tell myself, "Do what you know you can do." Measuring my talent to the seasoned stylists around me soon exposed how much proficiency I lacked, but I wasn't going out without a fight. I evaluated the client's hair and the desired style, then went to work. When I finally finished the client's hair, which seemed like forever, he seemed pleased but I could tell the owner of the salon was not satisfied with what she saw. At the end of the workday, she told me that she saw the potential, but she did not feel like I had the experience for that next level of work. Besides, I was too young to be working in a salon and she did not want to be fined by the State Board.

I thought I would be offended but I was not. Instead of getting discouraged and quitting, I was even more inspired to pursue my dream. If at the age of sixteen, I could get that kind of opportunity, how many more opportunities would I get if I invested more in my equipment and skills? I was resolved that if I ever received an opportunity to work in a barbershop or salon again, my skills or preparation would not be a factor. Someone once told me early in my journey that preparation plus opportunity equals success. That is such a true statement. You can have all the opportunities in the world but if you are not prepared you can potentially squander a once in a lifetime opportunity. A door had been opened and I was grateful for the chance to learn that I was lacking. Then an even bigger door opened for me.

Business was booming. By my senior year, I was much better than before and I had the clientele to prove it. Not only was I servicing many of my peers in the neighborhood, I was servicing my high school football coaches, principals and my coach's kids. There were times my teachers would give me passes to get out of class a little early to cut their hair in their office. For a high school kid, I was doing pretty well for myself. Unfortunately, I did not come up in the most financially secure environment. Making enough money to purchase many of the latest fashions for myself, keep a pair of the hottest shoes, and pay for my own lunch, felt pretty good. My newfound success started with two things: one, I invested in my dream and two, I was persistent. Once I knew barbering was what I wanted to do as a career, my mother told me to invest in the best equipment and that it would pay for itself later. That was some of the best advice she could have given me. When you have a God given vision such as the one I had to become one of the best barbers around, you should invest in it as much as you can and trust God to do what you cannot do. Secondly, the salon owner telling me I had skills but I was not quite ready for that level of work could have been a devastating deterrent. Keep in mind a closed door in some cases is an open opportunity in others. If I had never encountered that salon experience as early as I did, I may not have been as prepared for the blessing I had been walking in and the one that was to come. Being in the right place at the right time is an understatement in comparison to what I was about to experience.

Around 1994 my life changed. I was out of high school and cutting hair part-time at home while working my first corporate job. I was still cutting hair for my peers and former teachers after work and on the weekends. It was an ordinary day, in the basement of my best friend's home cutting his hair. This guy had been my best friend since the second grade and we're more like brothers. He was one of my first test dummies in the barber chair. After finishing his haircut, we were downstairs playing pool waiting for my next client. I had never met him and it turned out he was their cousin from New York.

My friend's older brother raced down the stairs and asked me if I was ready for my next client. There was such urgency in his voice when he instructed me not to mess this up. Well, that sparked a new series of emotions and curiosity. I began to wonder who this person from New York was that caused my friend to both question how prepared I was to service this guy. I was beginning to get a little offended because he knew my skills, potential and professionalism as a barber.

I was hit with an instant reality check. He proceeded to tell me that his cousin was the platinum recording artist Keith Sweat. Those infamous words "are you ready" were almost causing temporary paralysis. I felt like I was on trial all over again. If I only knew back then what I know now, when the Bible says in Matthew 24:44, *"Therefore you also be ready,"* I would not have been so nervous. However, I did not know that verse nor was I living the life of a born again believer, needless to say I was nervous. If I had been, I would have known there was no reason for me to be anxious because this was just the next opportunity that would thrust me to that next level in God.

Shortly after my friend told me whose hair I was about to cut, Keith Sweat walked down the stairs. I had never seen so much gold and diamonds on an individual in person. I felt like I had instantly arrived. Now, all I had to do was perform. It was one of the coolest experiences of my life. All my life, I envisioned being one of the best barbers around and having one or two really nice barbershops. Never in a million years did I imagine that I would be a "Celebrity Barber." Here I was, cutting my first celebrity's hair; not just any celebrity, but a major celebrity who just happened to be my best friend's cousin and just happened to stop by the house that day. What an opportunity!

I can testify that seminars are good. Instructional programs are helpful. Counsel and professional guidance is necessary; but when God orders your steps and he directs your path, that is priceless. There is no way I could have known we would move from the South Westside of Atlanta Georgia to the Eastside of DeKalb County when I was around seven years old. I would become best friends with my next-door neighbor and his older brother would be just like my older brother. We would grow up, leave high school, go on to college, start working and find out my best friend's cousin is a very successful R&B Artist. Nor could I know that I would be doing what I loved in his basement and from there my life would never be the same.

After that momentous occasion, I was never the same. My reputation within my community was unprecedented, I was a force to be reckoned with. Not so much because of what others thought of me, but because I had gained bragging rights that no one else had. I was a force to be reckoned with because of how I saw myself. I have never been one that followed the crowd. For me, having that opportunity did not make me arrogant but I became more humbled in many ways because I had been raised to believe in God. I was more humbled with this encounter because I knew I did not do anything to deserve it. I was not living for God, but I believed in my heart that God was real and one day I would turn my life around and live for Him. I was convinced even more of God's love and favor on my life. My talent to cut hair was God given, so when this unexpected door was opened it was just another way that God was showing me that I was on the right path. This is what gave me the confidence to believe in myself more and to believe that God's plan for my life was not solely predicated on my right, wrong, good or bad decisions.

This does not mean we have a license to do whatever we want and God approves. This means that God has a plan for each one of us and his grace and mercy is sufficient for us all. There is an appointed time for us all to receive what God has for us. Our actions can and will delay the process, but I have learned that the process inevitably produces progress.

My instant stardom would be somewhat short lived. It would be a year or so before I would ever cut Keith Sweat's hair again; but it did not matter. I had the notoriety of cutting his hair that one time and I was a part of the family. Not to mention there was a part of me that knew and believed I would have another opportunity to service him again.

This encounter was the motivation I needed to come out of my mother's downstairs area and find a barbershop or salon to work in. I knew I was on the rise and I needed a more professional environment to service the overwhelming clientele I perceived was to come. Many of us get discouraged when we get a taste of that next level of success but the fullness of that success is not realized. It may be a relationship that seems ideal, and then all of a sudden it is gone. You may feel blindsided wondering what did I do wrong. It may be a business deal that seemed impossible not to close and all of sudden it falls through.

I will give you an example of a friend of mine. He has a very successful business that brings in millions of dollars each year. He is one of my mentors when it comes to business. Well, he came to me just recently sharing with me how his company lost a bid on a job that he felt they were sure to get because of the reputation they already had in business. It came time to close the deal and he said they lost the deal because someone under bid them by millions of dollars. Quite naturally, he was a little disappointed but not defeated. One thing I can say about this guy, he is relentless when it comes to seeing his business succeed.

Fast forward a year later. The company that underbid my friend for the project for some reason lost the contract, and the bidding process was opened again. Needless to say, my friend put his bid in again. This time, not only did he win the bid, but his bid unplanned and unexpectedly came in millions of dollars lower than the lowest bidder.

God is omnipotent. A thousand years to God is as one day and a day is as a thousand years. He is not bound by time like we are. The only thing God is bound by is His word and His will for our life.

A year later, the opportunity to service Keith Sweat came again. My friend called me with the infamous question again, "Are you ready?" This time without hesitation, fear, or any anxiety I said, "Absolutely!" I was so excited. I knew this was my opportunity to represent my craft well and walk in the blessing I knew was for me. I showed up with my presentation on point, all my tools were finely tuned and I was ready for action. I remember walking up the stairs to this nice mansion honored for this opportunity on one hand and envisioning myself having this for myself one day on the other. I went into Keith's home, greeted him, set up my equipment and began to work.

I must say at this point I am a little nervous. Not about the finished product, but because I am in awe of what God had done in his life and what He is doing in my life. I had never been in a mansion like his before nor had I ever seen one like it other than on television and the movies. The moment arrives. I finish his haircut, gave him the mirror and the words that proceeded from his mouth would affirm my position as a "Celebrity Barber". He looked at the mirror, smiled and said, "That's alright. I may take you on the road with me." Twenty years later, I am still Keith Sweats personal barber and I have had the pleasure of servicing many other celebrities such as R&B group Bel, Biv, Devoe, Silk, LSG and more. I have been afforded the opportunity to service American Idol winner Reuben Studdard, also. I am very thankful for the opportunities that Keith Sweat has given me to service him for so many years but my biggest honor came when I received a phone call saying Muhammad Ali needed a haircut and I was the one requested to service him.

God can and will bless you in ways beyond your imagination. Joseph can testify better than any of us. He went from being his father's favorite child, to being thrown in a pit by his jealous brothers. He was sold into slavery, lied on by Potiphar's wife, thrown into jail, and betrayed by a fellow inmate. During the time of his slavery, there are two essential things in the story of Joseph that can keep us encouraged while in our process. The Bible says that God was with Joseph and God prospered him no matter where he was.

And the Lord was with Joseph, and he was a successful man...Genesis 39:2 NKJV

Society wants us to believe if we are not rich, if we are not living in our dream home, if we are not driving the nicest cars, or if we are not vacationing once a week we are not successful. All of these things are great to have and are good inspirations to keep us dreaming and reaching for higher accomplishments in life. However, success is not predicated upon obtaining or achieving these things alone. Success, fundamentally is moving closer and closer each day to your desired goal, and obtaining or achieving some encouraging nuggets along the way. Joseph's primary goal in life above all things was to do God's will. In slavery, he found a way to glorify God in his situation. When we do what God has called us to do regardless of how bleak it may seem, not only are we assured God is with us, but we can be assured he will prosper us.

Many of the things we go through in life are not about us. God is so much bigger than us and we should find honor in God using us where ever we are planted. We do not know what someone is going through and how you may have the very answer or inspiration they need to get through their situation. The Bible says that Joseph's master saw that the Lord was with him and that he was blessed.

And his master saw that the Lord was with him, and that the Lord made all that he did to prosper in his hand. Genesis 39:3. NKJV

Throughout his whole process, Joseph never gave up on God because he was secure in two things; who he was and whose he was. When you know you are a child of the Most High God and in Him you are more than a conqueror, you do not allow your present circumstances to define your future destiny. It is important that we embrace the gift of life each and every day and inspire someone along the way. You may have the answer someone needs to get through their moment of desperation. You may be the light someone has been waiting to see outside of all the others who have judged them or looked down on them for their less fortune. Last but not least, your destiny may be attached to your service and obedience while in your darkest moment. By the end of Joseph's journey he would be exalted second in command to Pharaoh. God can and will exalt you in due season.

I could have never imagined, that my gift and talent would open doors for me to connect with some of the most iconic figures in this world and befriend many of them along the way. Having the privilege to travel the world to places I thought I would only see on National Geographic is certainly a testimony that God can and will use anyone who makes themselves available for His purpose. I can assure you, what God has for you is for you. All He wants for you is to trust him in the good, the bad, and the indifferences because it is all a part of the process to get you to progress.

And we know that all things work together for good to those who love God, to those who are called according to His purpose. If God is for us, who can be against us? Romans 8:28,31 NKJV

CHAPTER 4
GOD HAS A PLAN

From 2011 to 2013, I faced three of the most challenging years of my life. In a later chapter I will tell you how I overcame the death of my father and my brother. But at this point in my life, neither my father's nor my brother's death compared to the pain, hurt, and disappointment I would endure in those years. Life was so dark and grim in those days. The bout I had with Tourette's syndrome as a child couldn't compare to that season and the dark force I was facing. During that time, I was so stressed and confused; I lost about 15 pounds; I was blindsided with some of the scariest information I would ever receive. To top it all off, my wife would come to me one day out of the blue to say she wasn't in love with me and didn't want our 12-year marriage anymore. I was stunned beyond reason. There was absolutely nothing that I could have foreseen that could have prepared me for this devastating news. I was not oblivious to the challenges in our marriage from the very beginning, and there was always a question of how deep her love was for me. But, at this point in our union I thought surely we had grown past all of the obstacles that would suggest divorce.   Clearly, from her words and her actions, it was evident she was already gone and I had absolutely no clue how to correct all that I was facing. My world was literally turned around and flipped upside-down. However, the one thing I can honestly share with you is this- when you are trusting God, He has the ability to keep you in perfect peace in the midst of any storm. God gave me a word of hope early in my trials that would carry me through the tests and difficulties of my life. I remember being by myself fasting and praying in a hotel in downtown Atlanta. I was broken, confused and out of my mind. I was seeking God for answers as to why my life was instantly changing, seemingly for the worst. I pleaded with Him asking when was He going to restore my joy, my peace, my kid's peace, and my marriage. It was then, I heard God just as clear as if I were speaking to myself say, *"Be still and know that I am God." Psalms 46:10 NKJV*. That word was my constant reminder that God not only heard my cry, but He was concerned about me and He was in control of the situation. I didn't know what challenges were ahead for me, but I remember leaving the hotel with my head up and my chest out knowing that regardless of the outcome, I was in His hands.

Returning home with the confidence of God and His word, and the well-being of my kids in mind, I felt like a lion walking in the wilderness alone. Prior to leaving for the hotel there was so much tension and hostility in my home. By this time, my wife was mentally, physically, spiritually and emotionally checked out of our marriage. I felt like I was contending with hell on earth every day. I am a lion at heart and the Lion of Judah is truly the inspiration of my life, but anyone that knows anything about the lion kingdom, a lion is esteemed primarily by his pride, and mine was dismantling. My marriage was at its worst. Like I said, my marriage was challenged from day one, but I thought we had a fairly decent life prior to 2011. As a matter fact, many people thought we had the ideal family. Business was good, ministry was going well, and most of all my family was healthy and happy, or so I thought. Little did I know there was a hidden trouble brewing within my marriage that would soon blind side me tremendously.

My wife and I met at a church we both attended back in 1998. I was fairly new to the church but it didn't take me long to realize she was the one I wanted to spend the rest of my life with. I would see her around church every week and we would speak occasionally and I would hear from friends of mine and hers that she was secretly inquiring about my current relationship status. In December of 1998, all of the inquiries made sense. She sent a message through one of her friends to invite me to a Christmas party held at her home. To this day, she still swears she didn't invite me, she says it was her friend that invited me. That's another book. Regardless of who invited me, it would be the start of a courtship that would lead to three kids and twelve years of marriage. I proposed to her within six months and we were married six months after that. We married in December 1999 and we had one of the most beautiful weddings. God's blessings were truly a part of the wedding planning and the ceremony. So many people blessed us with finances and gifts, many of our wedding expenses were covered from financial gifts alone. We were blessed to have a beautiful reception, all of our friends and family attended and enjoyed themselves and I was finally married to the women I believed I would spend the rest of my life with. Call me a hopeless romantic, but I thought life couldn't get any better. All the sacrifices I made to follow God, practice celibacy, and deny myself of the pleasures of women and clubs I thought had all paid off. I married the woman that I wanted to grow old with, have kids with and life would be a bed of roses. I would find out really quickly that this walk wasn't about me but it was about the purpose and plans God had for my life.

The second day of our honeymoon would set the tone for a journey that would produce everything but a bed of roses. My new wife disrupted the paradigm in which I thought our marriage was going to be built on. During the courtship, when we realized that we were serious about one another we both agreed that we would build our relationship on God, love, respect, family and honesty. Not too hard, right? Wrong! On the second day of our honeymoon, my wife decided this was a perfect time to confess to a blatant lie she told me during the wedding planning. I could not believe she waited until after we were married to confess this blatant fabrication and abuse of my trust. I won't disclose the nature of the lie but it was serious enough to make me reconsider my marriage to her. What made it worse, she had the audacity to get upset with me because I was upset. She had every opportunity to be straightforward and honest with me and she deliberately withheld information from me. I felt betrayed, slighted, and most of all, disrespected. Needless to say I was so taken back by this blatant disregard to me and my feelings, but because I believed this was the woman God called me to marry, I forgave her and attempted to move on from the transgression.

After we made it past that first hiccup, I felt we could work through things appropriately. Honestly, I contemplated annulling our marriage a few times because I couldn't understand the blatant disrespect and I was very offended. Still, I believed she was the woman God ordained for me so I embraced the truth of the matter. I was married to a beautiful, intelligent woman whom I loved and I thought truly loved me, and my marriage was worth fighting for.

She was a corporate woman doing well, working in a managerial position for a Fortune 500 company and I was an entrepreneur with a thriving career as a celebrity barber. It was a beautiful dance; I was privileged to tour the world with my clients. Life was thriving for the both of us. But the challenges of marriage didn't stop with that one incident. Our first three years of marriage were very rocky. What seemed to be a match made in heaven while we were dating, was taking the shape of hell on earth while we were married. The unforeseen attitude change was overwhelming; the adoration that was very prevalent during our courtship was now a figment of my imagination. It was all starting to weigh heavily on the respect and appreciation I had for my wife and the mother of my children. My wife gave birth to my daughter, (my baby girl) almost a year after we were married. Because I loved my wife, my kids, and the whole idea of being married, I was willing to push past the confusion of what was seemingly a drastic change of behavior. There was a tremendous shift in behavior from the time we were dating to the day we were married. I had my issues that I'm sure she would say contributed to her feeling justified in some of her ways. However, there is one thing any and every one that knows me will tell you about me, I am the same person in season and out. There is no mask in my life. I felt as if she took the mask off as soon as we were married.

On a side note, I had to ask myself, was she that good or was God shielding me for his higher calling? I now believe it was God shielding me for his higher calling. I don't profess to know everything but I am thankful for the gift of discernment. Because of the anointing of God that was on our family, our ministry and our business, I believe God shielded me from the issues that could have possibly hindered us from being together. I am almost certain, if I had clearly seen some of the character traits that were very offensive I wouldn't have been mature enough to accept God's plan for us to be united in marriage. Loving your wife as Christ loves the church essentially means you must press through the issues that come with two people that are totally different, have totally different views and a different set of unresolved circumstances. This is essentially what Christ did for us. He was not of this world and yet because of His undying love for us he clothed Himself in the filthy rags of humanity, that He might have a more in depth relationship with His creation.

For God made Christ, who never sinned, to be the offering for our sin, so that we could be made right with God through Christ.
2Corinthians 5:21 NLT

God is not the Author of confusion. All we can do as human beings striving to do God's will is be honest with who we are, surrender who we are to God, and allow Him to guide us through it all. I know I made mistakes in our marriage, but dishonesty wasn't one of them. I was honest with God myself and with my wife. Therefore, I had to trust if this is where God had me, there had to be a plan that's bigger than what I could see at the time. One thing I could see clearly is that God was blessing our family and He was using our family to be a blessing of hope and inspiration to so many others and that was enough for me to stand on.

CHAPTER 5
FACING MY BROTHER'S DEATH

The dishonesty, I would forgive and get over. The unnecessary attitude, I would press through. But over the years, the lack of respect and appreciation for me as her husband would soon take a turn for the worst. As I said earlier, life wasn't a bed of roses but it wasn't a bed of thorns either. By then, we had three beautiful kids, a profusion of friends and a blossoming ministry together. But whenever you enter into a marriage or any relationship with unresolved issues that are deeply rooted and heavily persuasive to your paradigm of thought, there is a concern of *when* we come into trouble, not *if.*

I am not trying to suggest we have to be perfect or the myth that most men often walk in "I have to get *it* out of my system (playing the games) first." No. To overcome many of the challenges that come with two people bonding together as one, simply means that you must be willing to operate in what I call Life's Triple A's: *Acknowledgement, Acceptance* and *Action*. Triple A is a local towing service that rescues you when you're stranded or your vehicle is broke down on the side of the road. My idea of life's Triple A service works in a similar way. No one is perfect, but before you can ever be any good for yourself or to anyone else, you must first be true to yourself. If we were to practice these "Triple A's" of life I believe we could rescue ourselves and our relationships when we arrive in a tight spot.

Acknowledgement of all your proclivities and the idiosyncrasies that influence you in a good or bad way is the first step to emotional freedom. When you're free to be you, and confident in how God created you, you don't just send forth your best representative, you send your true representative. This is the true you. So many of us thwart our opportunities to have healthy relationships, because we present ourselves as imposters to others. We do this as a result of fear of someone knowing who we really are and how inadequate we can potentially feel at times. The challenges of life create so many insecurities that cause us to mask our issues, simply because we know the trials, mistakes, and misfortunes that precede us don't necessarily define us, they make us better. So, instead of allowing your significant other, fiancé or spouse an opportunity to glimpse into the darkness that has been a part of your life experiences, you hide behind the facades of work, family, friends and successes. You never really expose some of the truths that have molded you into the man or woman you are today. However, God knows everything about us, the good, the bad, and the downright ugly and He loves us through it. Give the person you say you love an opportunity to love the real you--the good, the bad, and the ugly.

O Lord, you have searched me and known me! You know when I sit down and when I rise up; you discern my thoughts from afar. You search out my path and my lying down and are acquainted with all my ways. Psalms 139:1-3NKJV.

Before entering into a relationship an individual must be whole and healthy. Being whole and healthy doesn't mean you're *USDA* approved--*Universally, Satisfied, Decided, Accepted*; or that you've passed all of the socially accepted requirements. It simply means you are one with God and yourself, faults and all. When you accomplish this step, it is much easier to become one with yourself, align your steps in marriage, and with other relationships. That brings us to the next *"A"*, *Acceptance.*

Acceptance essentially means taking responsibility for what is yours. So many of us live behind masks and facades because we are too ashamed to deal with the reality of our past hurts, disappointments, deceptions, failures and other stifling mental and emotional disabilities. When we do this, we bring this façade of who we are to our relationships. We perpetuate these unrealistic ideals and expect the person we say we love to fix or help correct something he or she has not been exposed to. When you send your representative (the perfect unrealistic you) before you and not the essence of who you are (good, bad, sometimes ugly, broken, open for growth, at times insecure) self, you create the unhealthiest paradigm imaginable. Then you create unrealistic expectations, and when unrealistic expectations are un-met, you enable unhealthy relationships.

Early in my courtship with my wife, this is one of the things that confirmed within me that I would marry her. I remember wrestling with the idea of taking the leap of proposal. I was only twenty-four years old at the time. I had no kids, never married and not to mention, I was not a full year removed from clubbing, traveling, and living the good life as a celebrity barber. I knew the change that God brought in my life was real. I took that time of being single to become one with God and myself.

We were in church on a Sunday morning, and I remember the pastor preaching about people in relationships just needing to be honest. He said, women are not just looking for a man that looks good; they want someone that is honest. That word of inspiration really penetrated my spirit and I knew this would be another huge test for me. The Bible tells us *"...the righteousness of God is revealed from faith to faith..." Romans 1:17KJV*

I was good with myself and I was on the path to making the person I was better. But, I was not sure if she would be good with all of me. I knew I could not build a quality relationship on pretentiousness, much like the relationships I was previously in. If there was anything to further come from this relationship, I knew it had to be built on honesty and righteousness.

After church, I braced myself to share with her some of the harsh realities of my past that only God and my mother knew. I prepared myself to accept that if the harsh reality of my past was too much for her to bear, she and I would only be friends moving forward. We arrived at her home and I told her, I believed God had called her to be my wife and if that was true I must be totally honest with her. I went down the list of everything I deemed negative about myself. She was already endowed with all of my good (so I liked to believe). Like I said, most of us always send out our polished representative, but rarely do we ever expose the true person we are.

She took in everything I said, took a deep breath, and said, "Thank you for being honest and giving me the opportunity to make a clear decision." That was the biggest weight off my shoulders. At that point, it did not matter to me if we would only be friends after that, because I felt relieved knowing I was free to be me with her. We were married a few months later that year.

When you accept who you are and most importantly whose you are, you give the individual you desire to be with the opportunity to make a sound decision whether or not they want to accept you for who you are. When a person accepts you for who you are, they then take the responsibility to work with you as you work on you. Now "I" legitimately becomes "we". We all are a work in progress, but when you only allow your representative to be seen you delay the process of your progress. It's challenging to be a unified force when one person is masking or hiding internal issues. Instead of

49

having an affair with a third party on the outside, it's like having an affair with a third party on the inside. You must be open and transparent if you want to have successful relationships.

Action, the last "A" in the process. God designed us like a work of art, we are constantly being shaped and molded in the Master's hand. *"O house of Israel, can I do with you as this potter?" Jeremiah 18:6 NKJV.* We must intentionally and intensely contend with our logic of what we want people to see as opposed to who God has called us to be. We are a work in progress and God is doing His part to shape and mold our spirit man by way of our life experiences, the challenges we face, the highs and the lows we encounter, and the invaluable knowledge we obtain from encountered relationships. It's imperative that we actively address some of the not so attractive issues we have. I don't know about you but I want to be free to be me, not some pretentious representation of me. I remember being at the home of one of my R&B friends. We were in his studio and in walks this mega star actor to do an interview on his radio station. I was so honored to be in the midst of this multimillionnaire artist and actor. But outside of being elated to be in their presence, the one thing that blessed me the most was this. When the radio segment was over and everyone was expressing their gratitude and saying their goodbyes, the actor said something that helped reshape my approach to life, as it relates to what success looks like. As he was leaving he was thanking my friend for the interview and he shared these words, "It was refreshing to be myself unlike always performing in front of the camera".

This suggested to me, although he was very wealthy and according to American culture very successful, he didn't have many opportunities to be himself outside of the Hollywood image he had to constantly up-hold. This is not to suggest that he doesn't like his job, but it was clear he enjoyed being himself and not having to worry about paparazzi, or the media critiquing his every word and move.

During the interview, the actor was in rare form. You could tell he was comfortable, he was laughing, joking, having fun with all the callers and everyone in the studio. His job is to act so I understand why he does what he does. But not having the liberty to be yourself on a daily basis can be taxing and very cumbersome. If we take wisdom from his comment, we will see that acting or performing can be a form of bondage. He was so relieved to be himself for that moment just as I'm sure you will, when you take *action* and as they say "let your hair down." Be yourself. Insecurities are adapted persuasions that influence us to hide and mask our hurts and disappointments. But when you take the proper measures to heal from whatever has you feeling like you can't be honest to the world and move forward in a positive way, not only will God give you the courage to be you, but He will put people in your path that will love you for you and assist you as you work on you. It's not healthy to live a life where you don't feel free to be yourself, especially when you've set the standards by masking many of your proclivities. When God created you He created a unique individual and you must embrace the challenges of life that have helped to shape you into the beautiful and exquisite person you are. God said that we are fearfully and wonderfully made. *Psalms 139:14 KJV*. Once we give our life to God we don't have to mask who we are. We have been redeemed, old things are passed away, behold all things have become new. *2 Corinthians 5:17KJV*

CHAPTER 6
OVERCOMING MY BROTHER'S DEATH

It was February 2003. Our home was the meeting ground for most fellowships. We hosted a New Year's Eve breakfast every year, birthday celebrations, wedding proposals. You name it; we were always hosting something at our home. One of the most common gatherings we would have were card parties. Our family and friends would come over almost every weekend and we would play cards all night. This particular night was no different from the rest. My wife and I always played together. She and I were playing against two other people when the phone rang. I answered the phone. It was my brother on the other end.

Allow me a moment to give you a quick backdrop to my brother's life. My brother was about seven years my senior. Ironically, my brother and wife went to high school together and didn't realize it until the day of our wedding.

He was someone I looked up to for many years. We came up occasionally fighting (of course I was on the losing end), playing, arguing like siblings do and we struggled as a family in many ways. My brother was truly my big brother. I didn't have many worries in the neighborhood because many of his peers respected him and watched out for me because of the respect they had for him. He was an extremely gifted sculptor, he was someone you always knew could and would be successful with anything he set his mind to do. Drugs, however, would rob him of all the potential he had to be as successful as he could have been.

My mother and I along with many others had prayed and fought with my brother for many years to help him get off drugs. He would have times of successful rehabs for weeks, months, and sometimes years. But we would never see him fully overcome the battle with drugs in this life.

On the night of our card party, when the phone call came in, I could tell he was high on drugs. He was asking me to come pick him up from the drug house because they were trying to kill him. This was nothing new, my mom and I heard this line many times before. Sometimes it had some truth but many times it was a play on our emotions to get what he wanted from us. This night seemed different, though. So, I took his call and I told him I was not coming out to pick him up. He would hang up and call again asking me to come pick him up, and again I would say no. This particular night I was led to be a bit more sensitive to the situation for a couple of reasons.

My brother and I had a major blow-up the night before. We hadn't had a confrontation like that since we were kids. This particular day he was high on drugs and he had broken into my mother's home. Scared and concerned because of his behavior, she called me over to try and persuade him to leave her home. His refusal to leave made me more furious. I was already angry with the level of disrespect he was displaying in the presence of my mother and my grandmother. I verbally snapped! I said some things to him out of anger that I truly regretted. After the altercation, I returned home very grieved. I was so broken seeing my brother in the state he was in, knowing, prior to the these last few weeks he had been clean from drugs for a very long time and he had just started a really good job. A part of me really wanted to make myself available to him for his comfort.

Yelling at him was so outside of my character. Not only did I want to be there for him, but that was my way of repenting for my actions and assuring him that I loved him and I wanted to be there for him. Before hanging up for the second time, I said "I love you bro, but I can't come to get you". His reply grieves me even now as I attempt to put my thoughts to paper. He paused for a second and muffled "I know. I love you too."

Let me share with you why that was so profound. All the years of our lives, my brother and I made this silly pact when we were younger that we wouldn't say the words "I love you". We weren't raised like that. We didn't hear the words I love you in our home or in our family. It was clear that our mom loved us and would do anything in the world for us, but actually using the words "I love you" in our household was foreign. So, my brother and I made this pact, instead of saying the actual words we would make some silly verbal gesture that was our code of saying "I love you". We did this well into our adult years. This night when I impulsively said it and he responded in the same manner, I felt something different about that moment. He called a third time and that time would change the perspective of my relationship with my wife for many years.

The phone rang and when I reached to answer it, my wife in haste, grabbed the phone before I could answer it. She proceeded to speak for me, as if she didn't have the confidence that I would speak for myself. Or, as if I wouldn't make the responsible decision for my family and not leave my home to go rescue my brother in this drug infested area. My mind was already made up that I wasn't going, but I felt that it was imperative that I made myself available for him because there was something different about that night. When I heard her saying to my brother, "He is not coming. We love you, but he is not coming", I was infuriated that she didn't respect my leadership enough to allow me to make the final decision. That was the last time my brother would call, and that was the last time I would ever hear from him again. The next phone call came around three o'clock the following morning. It was my mother telling my wife that my brother had been shot by the police.

CHAPTER 7
DISCONNECTED BUT DETERMINED

After my brother's death, I went into an immediate tailspin. All the questions ran through my mind. What could have I done differently? What should have I done differently? Of course, there was no reasonable solution that would bring my brother back. Therefore, I felt like I was left with one resolve; there was one thing I could do differently. I could not bring my brother back; I could not erase the guilt of not being there for him the night of him calling. I could not erase the guilt of the many times before when I did not allow him to come over simply because I didn't want to deal with the conflict of my wife not understanding him as I did. There was one thing I felt I could do. I could shut off my emotions toward my wife. And though I vowed that I would never commit adultery nor would I divorce her because I did not want to dishonor God or my marriage in that manner, I also vowed, that I would never give her that much of my heart again to hurt.

This would be the beginning of an uphill journey for her for many years and a downward spiral for me and our relationship. I now realize she had only reacted out of her own fears and insecurities. She was doing what she believed would protect her family and keep us safe. But at that time, no amount of reasoning could suffice the pain of losing my brother. I became so disconnected because I honestly did not know what else to do. I knew I could not continue to subject my heart to her neglect. What else was I supposed to do? I would ask myself this question over and over for many years, which in return would be my first mistake. I was so hurt and angry, I didn't think to ask God what to do. I made up in my mind, I really didn't want God to do anything different. My brother was gone and there was nothing I could do about it. I was married to someone that I was furious with, compiled with the fact I never felt that she had the love for me that I had for her, so I was content with being guarded from then on out.

My kids were babies; divorce was not an option for me. Abandoning my family was not an option, and I conceptualized there was nothing else I could do that was morally responsible but fight through my pain. The only resolve I found was to shut down and not look to her any longer to be an emotional support for me.

As a human being trying to balance the biblical and spiritual truths with the harsh realities of life, we do not always get it right. I can honestly share with you in my quest to live a righteous lifestyle, the decision to block my emotions from my wife may not have been the best decision to make. Although it shielded me from not being so let down and disappointed when she did not respond to me in ways I thought a wife should, it led me down a road that was unbecoming of how I viewed myself. I would become very indifferent in my relationship and I did not realize that was happening until it was seemingly too late. The Bible tells us:

For we do not wrestle against flesh and blood, but against principalities, against powers, against the rulers of the darkness of this age, against spiritual hosts of wickedness in the heavenly places.
Ephesians 6:12. NKJV

Life can and will throw us curves balls. Sometimes those that are closest to us hurt us the most. Jesus' disciples betrayed Him, His own people crucified Him, and one of His dearest disciples, Peter, denied even knowing Him. But, Jesus never allowed His heart to turn against any of them. The lion in me, the man my father influenced me to be, the environment I was raised in, even the culture that influenced my perception, persuaded me to respond the way I did. When essentially I should have relied more on the Word of God "love your wife as Christ loved the church." The Bible also instructs us to love as He loves because it covers the multitude of sins. I heard a preacher and world leader say something to this effect, "We are not human beings having a spiritual experience, we are spiritual beings having a human encounter."

Living for God is a lifestyle that is defined by our influences. This is why it is imperative to surround yourself with people who are and have been where you desire to go and to constantly feed yourself with information that will help you better the person you know you are called to be. Therefore, when you fall you will not be cast down because you have a point of reference that will guide you in the right direction. Although I was striving to be a righteous husband, father, and friend I was not addressing my indifference toward my wife.

I embraced this to be the very thing that was working, even though I knew deep down it was not God's best. In 2009, things would begin to unfold. By then years had passed since my brother's death. Life was bearable but not as emotionally profitable as it could have been. We were both ministering, loving our kids everyday but never fully addressing the deeper matters of the heart.

I traveled to Japan on a three-week trip with one of my celebrity clients and the crew. When I left home, I left with the same thought in mind I had the many other times I would travel. I was going to do my job, have fun, and come back the same way I left. Everyone in our crew respected my relationship with God. Many of them would ask me from time to time to pray for them, and they would ask me to counsel them concerning some of their pressing concerns. Some would even call me Rev or Pastor long before I came into the role of an ordained reverend. This made my relationship with my job more purposeful. I knew when I was out there on the road I was not just representing what I do for a living, I was representing the

God of purpose. Little did I know, I was about to be challenged in a way like none I had ever experienced in my Christian walk. My indifference was about to expose my inadequacies outside of God's favor.

Around the end of the second week in Japan, a young lady that was a part of our crew called my room and asked if I would join her for breakfast. Nothing wrong with that. Right? WRONG! First mistake. I am married, and this woman has all the appealing attributes that most men would desire in a woman. And deep down I heard that little small voice saying, "This may not be wise." Allow me to be clear. Two people of the opposite sex having breakfast, lunch or engaged in a social type of gathering is not necessarily wrong. However, you must ask yourself, "is it wise?" I did not know her situation but I knew my situation. I knew my marriage was at an emotional deficit and having breakfast alone with this talented and attractive woman could possibly influence me in a way I had not experienced in over ten years. Going against my spiritual instincts, responding to the flattering invite, I agreed to have breakfast.

We were having a nice, casual, cordial breakfast when she dropped the question on me. "How is it there are several men on this trip with us and only a few women and all of the women are after you?" Needless to say my ego went from zero to ten instantly. Here it is, I did not have to do much of anything to impress these women other than be myself. And one of the nicest ladies on the trip is admiring me enough to act on it.

The enemy knows how to strategically set us up for failure. The Word of God says the enemy is lurking for whom he can kill, steal, and destroy. I was not only flattered to know this young lady in particular was attracted to me but the other ladies on the trip were also. I was so far removed from the lifestyle of dating and flirting that I almost forgot how it felt to really be desired by a member of the opposite sex. When I gave my life to Christ, it was my pleasure to focus on nothing other than my relationship with God and my family. This is why it is important for couples to always be intentional to date, show affection and admiration to your spouse, because if you don't, trust me, someone will. Test and temptations of life are not so much about people; it is more about the enemy trying to derail you from your assignment. If you trust God and give the test and temptation to Him He will use it for your good.

My brethren, count it all joy when you fall into various trials, knowing that the testing of your faith produces patience. But let patience have its perfect work… James 1:2-3NKJV

That breakfast was the open door for this young lady and I to begin a friendship that would lend an ear for us to converse on a more personal level. She began to share in-depth and personal things pertaining to her life and I would do the same. All the while I was at war. Everything in me was telling me to pull back with the conversation before things go too far, but all the while I could not deny how good it felt to be admired and appreciated again by someone of the opposite sex. It all came to a head a couple of nights before leaving Japan.

I'll never forget the night we returned to the hotel from the show. She and I went back to my room to talk. There was an exchange of glances and subtle flirtatious comments. We were up all night talking and wrestling with the lust of our flesh. It was not until she made a comment that quickened my spirit to look at the bigger picture. She said in the midst of us both warring with doing the right thing "You are a genuine person." Then she said, "I wouldn't want to fall with you, your anointing is very attractive." I was so humbled. While I was allowing my flesh to be flattered by her words and attraction I was missing the bigger picture. As I mentioned earlier, I didn't know her situation I only knew mine.

After hours of conversation, I would find out she had voids in her life she was trying to fill as well. She did not need someone that would do what everyone else does, by giving in to the temptations of the flesh. She needed someone that would show her something different. She needed to see God. As the saying goes, "hurt people, hurt people." Because we were both challenged with our current situation, we were allowing our pain to draw us closer to one another as opposed to allowing the God in us to draw us closer to His Word. I thank God for His grace and His mercy, her comment created an opportunity for me to look deeper within myself. It helped me to see I was setting myself up for failure. I brushed myself off, said goodnight, bowed down and asked God for forgiveness. I returned from Japan unmarred by our conversation, feeling somewhat triumphant that a moment of attraction didn't manifest into a lifetime of destruction.

I believe because I contended with my flesh and allowed God to keep me from going as far as my flesh wanted go, she was able to see God in me. Not only was she able to see the God in me, but I was able to see how much more God wanted to use me in different arenas. That experience allowed me to see that my indifference was attracting unwanted attention and I needed to correct it. Something else would take place before I would finally make the turn.

CHAPTER 8
ANOTHER INAPPROPRIATE
ENCOUNTER

I returned home from Japan feeling both victorious and defeated. I felt victorious because I knew that it was the hand of God that kept us from doing the unthinkable and in spite of my battle with my flesh she saw the God in me. I was feeling defeated for two reasons. The first, I could not believe I had allowed myself to go there with this young lady. Up until that point I had been physically and emotionally faithful to my wife and then I had allowed myself to become physically and emotionally attracted to someone else. The second was that I had to contend with the attraction I was having for another woman and the disconnect that was continuously prevalent in my home.

Returning to Atlanta, Georgia, my wife and kids would always meet me at the airport. That was typically a beautiful experience from a long trip. Walking out of the airport to be met by my wife and kids greeting me with the biggest smiles and hugs was the most rewarding thing. I love dogs, so I understand why they say a dog is a man's best friend, because they greet you in the same manner (maybe with a lot more drool and biting). But there is nothing like being greeted with the love of family. I arrived home to see that while I was gone for two weeks my wife was on mission impossible. She had remodeled almost the whole house while I was gone. I was shocked, thrown back, and convicted. On one hand I should have been full of joy and excitement, because I knew this was my wife's way of surprising me and acknowledging our current disconnect. She was known for doing extravagant things like that and in times past it would remove any frustrations or aggravations I had towards her. This time was different and we both noticed it. Before I left to go to Japan I was already disappointed with my wife's concerns for my needs. Two weeks prior to me leaving to go to Japan, I would reach out to her in an effort to communicate my challenges with the level of our intimacy. Her communication to me was without empathy and instead of her showing any concern for my needs, she became more disconnected. Needless to say, her common demonstrative gestures did not have the same effect.

When I did not respond in the common manner of excitement she was accustomed to, it provoked her to ask me the question, did I do anything to defile our relationship while I was gone. Initially, I told her no. Typical man's response or even a woman who is not ready to deal with themselves. However, God is all about truth and "the truth shall make you free". Eventually the guilt ate at me and I confessed my encounter with the young lady to her. I believed my honesty would help my situation, but it continued to make it worse. From my perspective anyway. When she did not say, "Oh, honey I am so glad you did not do what you could have done." Or "I understand how I may have influenced your behavior with my actions before you left." I did not get any of that. Instead I received more condemnation for defiling our marriage. Not to mention how frustrating it was to know that I was being honest about the encounter with this young lady and she did not believe me. In my mind, I felt my actions were justifiable based on her actions before I left. As I said earlier, unrealistic expectations bring about unmet expectations. It was unrealistic for me to think she would respond in the way I desired her to respond; an individual has the right to respond in the way they feel based on their perspective. It was also not realistic for me to expect anything different from her when throughout our marriage it was always challenging for her to be apologetic. Not to mention it is imperative for an individual to own their portion of the discord 100%, to provoke a positive change. When you marry you become as one, however it is God's job to bring conviction to us and our job to respond to that conviction. I don't know if God was convicting her or if she was not responding to His conviction. I know I was convicted, and it was my responsibility to address my disposition.

Her response did not help my situation. Once again, I felt like I could not win with her and my victorious moment was short lived. So what did I do? Instead of suppressing my feelings for this young lady I began having casual conversations with her, telling myself it was necessary to ease my frustration. And then disaster occurred. One that would set me on a path for the better.

CHAPTER 9
FALLING INTO VICTORY

The incident with the young lady would soon be swept under the rug like many of our other challenges. Even though it was not a concern that I would have had a sexual affair with this young lady, I would continue to talk to her without my wife knowing. That was literally a disaster waiting to happen.

It was our custom to go to Florida for family vacation every year. After arriving in Florida, we went to Universal Studios. We were having a great time riding the different rides, eating, taking pictures and enjoying everything that comes with the Universal experience. We came to this ride called Disaster. While in line waiting to get on the ride I had the grand idea to jump over the railings with no hands. My son's friend and I had been doing this in other lines we were waiting in. Feeling pretty good about my physical condition, not concerned with the height of the rail and without thought, I attempted to jump over the rail. In the blink of an eye, a disaster happened. I fell and broke my right radius.

For many of you, you may think it was just a disappointing incident or an unfortunate accident. For me, it was life changing. I had been cutting hair since I was fourteen years old. I worked in my first barbershop when I was sixteen and now I am a well-established "Celebrity Barber." This had been my career for over eighteen years. In an instant, my life was perceivably turned upside down. As I am picking myself up off the ground, looking at my mangled arm, for an instant, I thought my career was possibly over. But surprisingly, just as quick as that thought came it was replaced with contentment. I was not discouraged about breaking my arm. I was more concerned with making sure my wife and kids were not too devastated with my misfortune. That's the nature of who I am, I knew this was God snatching my attention. Once again, I would be mortified by wife's reaction to one of my most vulnerable moments. Picking myself up off the ground, bracing myself to deal with the embarrassment of the crowd, I walked over to my wife and kids clutching my right arm in agony to hear her say, "That's your cutting hand isn't it!" I could not believe those were the first words that would be uttered from her lips.

Her response sent me into a mental head-spin. On one hand I could not believe she would be that intolerant in such a detrimental moment, and on the other hand I knew I had to trust God because I was losing and I was losing bad. The ambulance came and got me and rushed me to the hospital. After X-rays, it was established that my right radius was broken in half and it required immediate emergency surgery.

When the surgeon arrived and told me his name, it was further confirmed my experience was a divine encounter with God. My surgeon shared one of the names that Jesus is known by. When he introduced himself, he said "My name is Dr. Messieh." Then he said "Like Messiah, just not spelled the same." When he walked out of the room all I could do was cry and worship God. I was having my own Jacob experience with God. I knew God wanted more from me and I knew he wanted me to forgive my wife for her actions from the beginning of our marriage, my brother's death, and now this inconsiderate reply. Like Jacob, I was wrestling with God. I wanted to do right by my wife and give her the love and adoration I knew she deserved, but I was so angry. In many ways, I felt like I had been bamboozled. I told God that I needed Him to change my heart. Just like the blessing of Jacob came at the breaking of his hip, my blessing came at the breaking of my arm.

In those weeks of being disabled and not being able to do the job that came so natural for me, I learned to trust God for strength, wisdom, provision, and knowledge. He truly provided. I would apologize to my wife for my previous behavior and I stopped all communications with the young lady from Japan. Even though there were some things about my wife's personality that I still had issues with, I started focusing more on her good and addressing more of my faults. I was taking *action*.

Essentially, our purpose in life is to be an advocate for positive change and to give God glory in everything we do. God will use anything to get us aligned with the plans he has for our life.

For I know the thoughts that I think toward you, saith the Lord, thoughts of peace, and not of evil, to give you an expected end.
Jeremiah 29:11KJV

CHAPTER 10
ALL HELL BREAKS LOSE

Now that I have started looking at myself and taking responsibility for my own actions, I am thinking surely everything it is about to turn around for the good. WRONG again. Before things would truly turn around, God allowed me to experience yet another test. I shared with you earlier that the Luke's home was something like an adult fraternity house. We hosted everything; New Year's Breakfast, Christmas, Thanksgiving, Labor day cookouts, and the like. You name it; we were hosting it. It was common for people to befriend and confide in us with many of their concerns. We were counselors and ministers at our church so it was easy for us to shift between friend, counselor and spiritual confidantes with everyone.

There was a particular couple that fellowshipped with us. My wife was closer with the wife than I was with her husband. All in all, they were friends of our family just like everyone else. Well, one day all that would change. While I was working, I received an interesting text from the wife asking if I was alone and able to talk. Now I am a firm believer the Spirit of God will convict and grieve you in some way when a situation is not quite right. Some may call it instinct, intuition, or your conscience. Whatever you call it, when I viewed the text, I felt it. The level to which you are tuned in to the Spirit and that inward Voice will determine how well you can hear and decide what that Voice is saying.

I heard the Voice, but there were a couple of things warring within. I was in disbelief that she could possibly be attempting what I thought she was about to attempt. She was married, and she was our friend. I am not a naive type of person but I try to give a person the benefit of the doubt, and I did not want to believe there was an agenda behind the text message. I was trying to be optimistic. I wanted to believe I was seeing more than was there. I was still on the edge of confronting my indifference with my wife and longing for that attention that I rightfully thought I deserved. I was changing for the better and it seemed as if she was staying the same. A part of me wanted to see if my inclination was accurate.

I realize I should have been like Elijah and listened to that still small voice. But when an individual is not fully surrendering his will to God, his natural proclivities have the propensity to influence him in ways that are unbecoming to who he is and who he represents. In this case, my ego was influencing me to investigate the scenario further rather than immediately neutralizing the distraction.

I responded to her text message that I was available. The young lady called me and began to have small talk. It was almost immediately that I began to feel the conviction. I had a strong inclination where this conversation was going and I knew this was not a position I wanted to be in again; especially with someone we considered a friend. She proceeded to tell me she had a confession to make. She said she was attracted to me, and had a desire to be with me. She went on to say she knew it was wrong but she could not help what she liked. Flattered, confused, and a bit baffled, before addressing her statement I asked her if there was anything that I had done in the past that may have influenced her to approach me in this manner. Outside of all the carnal feelings I was having, I knew it was wrong to be entertaining this conversation and I was genuinely caught off guard. I did not recall ever doing anything that would open the door for her to feel this way. I was sure I hadn't done anything that would cause her to have the confidence to approach me with her feelings. I asked that question with one thing in mind, I wanted to know what my error may have been in the matter. Instead of getting relief from any negligence of my own, the flattery went deeper.

She said there was nothing I did to influence her other than being myself. Wow! Now, I hope the transparency that I am about to share with you challenges you to understand the battle of humanity and spirit and not judge as if this could never happen to you. Trust me, I have come to realize many things I thought could never happen, can and will happen if you do not keep your focus on God. The Bible instructs a man "not to think of himself more highly than he ought to think, but to think soberly…" *Romans 12:3 NKJV*

As a married man, a minister of the gospel, and a man that strives to live with integrity, I would love to tell you that when this woman approached me in that manner that I was sick to my stomach. But I cannot. At that moment, I was not. I'm not speaking on this matter proudly, but I believe it is imperative for us to understand that being a disciple for Christ is not a superficial journey. It is a spiritual journey encountered by human realities.

Remember, the first step to conquering our human inadequacies is to *acknowledge* they exist. Our strength and our message being heard and received is not all wrapped up in the profound orators we are, nor is it always received by unblemished walks we've obtained since turning our lives over to Christ. Many times our strength and our message comes from the times when you know that if it had not been for the Holy Spirit holding on to you, whispering in your ear, yelling at times, you, just like any other mortal being could and would have fallen. For a moment, I was really struggling with not entertaining the suggestions being thrown my way. There was a great void in my marriage as it relates to intimacy and I was still a bit vulnerable to the flesh from my encounter in Japan.

However, I am a witness that God will create room for an escape (*1 Corinthians 10:13*), even when you may not want it. I shook it off and told her I could not allow anything to go any further than that conversation. She said she agreed and she understood. I was still a bit thrown back by this challenging predicament. I suggested that we keep it between us since the situation did not go as far as it could have gone. There was no need to disrupt the paradigm we were currently living in. At the time, I figured since our feelings were able to be expressed and nothing other than an inappropriate conversation would come out of this encounter, there was no need to get anyone else involved. Wrong! I would soon find out you cannot allow inappropriate situations to linger in your life when God is trying to take you to the next level. That was especially the case for me. It was not in my character to keep those kind of secrets from my wife. I was so convicted, I felt like this young lady and I had our own dirty little secret. On top of that, from my perspective, I believed to some degree, I was innocent. God would later show me how I was not as innocent as I had convinced myself. At the time, I did not see any reason to keep that kind of secret from my wife that could possibly come back to haunt me later, but I'll never forget how it all came out.

A couple of weeks had gone by and I was wrestling with what I should do. Should I tell my wife what happened or do I let it go? I confided in a good friend of mine to see what I should do. Normally, when I go to him he is able to give me some fairly concrete advice. This particular day he had nothing. He told me I was in a tough spot and that I should pray about what to do. Many times we know what God is nudging us to do but because we want someone to talk us out of it or even to co-sign with us, we seek information from others when God has already given us the answers we need. One night after my wife and I were leaving a counseling session, I knew I had to tell her.

You remember earlier when I said God would show me I was not as innocent as I perceived myself to be. Well, God showed me, me. During that time, I allowed myself to become indifferent and emotionally disconnected with my wife, I was subconsciously subjecting myself to others in the world who were consequently dealing with similar if not the same things I was dealing with. Everything we go through in life is a manifestation of what has or is happening in the spirit world. I was physically and emotionally disconnected for so long, subconsciously I was putting off that aura to others that may have been struggling in their own way. The young lady I was having inappropriate conversations with in Japan was going through similar challenges in her life. Jesus says *"You will know them by their fruits..."* Matthew 7:16 NKJV. We are spiritual beings having an earthly encounter. Although I was doing many good things in the name of The Lord, I was not addressing the issue of indifference as I should have and it was manifesting itself in the people who were being drawn and connected to me. I was allowing a bad fruit to hang on a tree in my thoughts, instead of plucking it off.

We are challenged with sin and hardship because of the fall of Adam and Eve. Not necessarily because of anything we have done. Even though I did not do anything intentionally or directly to suggest to this young lady I was open for that type of affair, the state of my emotional disconnect was very apparent to someone who was having her own personal struggles. Like attracts like and deep calls to deep.

I took inventory, and once again, owned my piece of the pie. I opened up and shared everything with my wife. I couldn't be offended any longer with the young lady, because the errors of my ways were too prevalent. She had to be accountable for own actions, but I believed I had to be accountable for mine. This was one of those situations that could have possibly been avoided if I had addressed my issues of disconnect and indifference much sooner. After sharing with my wife what happened between me and the young lady and apologizing for my disconnect, her response would lead me to believe we were on our way to being an unstoppable force.

I did not tell her initially who the young lady was but when I finally told her she went through a whirlwind of emotions. She was angry, hurt, confused, baffled, and angry again. She felt so betrayed, rightfully so. But the words that proceeded out of her mouth assured me that none of this journey was in vain. With much boldness and assurance, she gave me a high five, looked me in the eyes, and said, "You are the man! I have so much respect for you because you didn't have to tell me." Everything I had been longing to hear and feel from my wife from the beginning of our marriage was solidified in that moment with those words. Let me remind you, I was married to a strong, intelligent, hardworking, independent, attractive sister. I was bracing myself for the worst. To hear those words of affirmation were an assurance to me that God was doing a new thing in our relationship.

FRANK LUKE

CHAPTER 11
AT THE END OF THE DAY

The one thing that I have come to learn about life is that there are no absolutes. Just like the mammoth sized monuments and buildings made by man's hands can be reduced to rubble, people are also broken by those same hands. It is impossible to determine when and if that building's infrastructure will shift just the same as if a person will shift in behavior. As it relates to infrastructures, some shifts are good, it's called getting settled. There are also some shifts that are not good; they actually cause things to collapse. Just as men rebuild broken structures bigger and better than ever, God does even better when men and women give their broken spirits over to His master plan.

The shift that came in my life at the end of 2010 was like the worst earthquake I would ever experience. The shift was so severe it rattled the foundation of my faith, destroyed the infrastructure of my marriage, offset the balance of my kids, and at the same time birthed a newfound purpose in God.

I thought for sure, after confessing to the inappropriate communication between the young lady and I, taking ownership of my actions, and hearing those words from my wife spoken with such passion, that my marriage was surely on the rise. I was very optimistic for a fresh start and I was content with moving past all of the faults we laid at each other's feet throughout the previous years. I had a newfound love for my wife.

One of the issues she had with me in the earlier years of our marriage was that I didn't support her desire to go back to school and finish her degree. All the time she had wanted to go back to school, I can admit my resistance was a little selfish. I thought I had already sacrificed a great deal to make her happy. We had little kids, and I was already longing for her to be more affectionately and intimately into me, as I was to her. I felt that her going back to school would just be one more thing that would justify her not giving me the attention I deserved from her, that was missing for the majority of our marriage. Well, now I was beyond those selfish thoughts. She was enrolled in school and she had my total support.

For a couple of months, we were making progressive steps to a better relationship. We were really striving to rise above all of the challenges we had faced the previous years of our marriage. All of that would soon change.

My wife had started working a new job, she was in school full time, and she had decided on top of that she was going to pledge a sorority. Although I had my reservations concerning the time she was spending (or not) with the family, I was dedicated to supporting her in this journey. There were many days I felt like I was a single parent. There were so many days the kids did not see her in the morning before going to school because she was working and they did not see her at night before going to bed because she was going to school and pledging. She would leave for work early in the morning, go to school after work, and participate in her sorority affairs after school. To this day, I'm amazed how she was able to do all of that and graduate with honors. Needless to say, she did not have to worry about home. I was working every day; I made sure the kids were taken care of with going to school, homework, food, and extracurricular activities. The chief thing for me was for her to recognize I was wholeheartedly supporting her going back to school and my family being unified was most important. I didn't fully support the sorority endeavor because I didn't fully understand it. Still, I accepted that's what she wanted to do so I supported her in that.

Spending the extra time with the kids was not that challenging for me. My kids have always been jewels to me. They will tell you, I can at times be just as big of a kid as they are. I have always coached my kids in sports, participated in school functions and more. I was more proud of myself that I wasn't being selfish and that I was one hundred percent on board with my wife getting her degree. God was doing a new thing in my heart. I was engaged in what I believed to be a newfound hope. It was so disheartening how she would receive my support and it was even more devastating what she would say to me around the end of 2010.

With past issues behind us and marriage perceivably moving forward, my wife dropped the unexpected bomb on me. She came to me shortly after our eleventh year anniversary and uttered these dreadful words to me. *I do not want to be married to you anymore. I am not in love with you.* She went on to tell me that in all the years we had been married, she had never been in love with me like that. With tears in her eyes, she seemingly opened the pages of a journal that had been tucked so deeply away in her heart, that it hurt her to even reveal them.

If I were a cartoon character, my mouth would have literally hit the floor in disbelief. In all that we had been through together, here we were with the stage set for us to climb higher in marriage than we had ever been before. We were finally on the same page headed down the same path, and she declared she wanted out. There was nothing that could have prepared me for what had just taken place. Throughout the entire marriage, we had our challenges and there were many times I was challenged with believing in whether the love she professed for me was genuine or not.

Periodically, I would say to her that I didn't believe she loved me as much as she led me to believe in the beginning of our courtship. Many times she would dismiss my feelings as untruths. Even with my doubts, there were a few things I always banked on because of both of our spiritual commitment to God. I always believed that no matter what happened in our marriage, I would never have a sexual affair, I would never physically abuse her and I would never divorce her. As life would have it, those *never* lines would be confronted and crossed.

I knew a genuine shift had taken place in my life to get me back to the loving, caring, supportive husband God called me to be when I asked for her hand in marriage. The man that was getting lost in indifference was dead and buried. I was determined to not let her words, actions or even my idiosyncrasies detour me from standing on the promises of God that were intended for my family. After she told me she did not want the marriage anymore I relentlessly began to pursue God to save my marriage. After all, she was the one that would always say "I want my husband back," implying she wanted the loving, optimistic, and caring husband she married in 1999, not the indifferent man I had become. Now that she had him, she didn't want him.

She would put forth some effort to salvage our marriage, but for the most part she was very consistent with telling me she was not in love with me and she wanted out. Quite naturally, I had my suspicions that the sudden shift and determination to move on had more to do with outside influences and not just her lack of desire to be married. I questioned and challenged her, whether there was anyone or anything else influencing her decisions and she would vehemently suggest that her decisions had nothing to do with anyone or anything else. She said her decisions were solely predicated on her lack of intimate attraction, lack of adoration, and she felt that she deserved more than what I was offering her. Allow me a quick moment to shift. One thing I have learned to embrace;

God is not blindsided by the things that blindside us. He is an omniscient God; He sees and knows all things.

For all that is secret will eventually be brought into the open, and everything that is concealed will be brought to light and made known to all. Luke 8:17 NLT

CHAPTER 12
A TURN FOR THE WORSE

By March 2011, everything took a turn for the worst. Frustration had built up on both sides, particularly mine. I was doing everything I knew to do to show my support for my wife going to school full-time and pledging. All the while, I was suffering trying to shield the kids from the internal shift that was tearing down the infrastructure of our family. My seeking God for strength, wisdom and restoration of my marriage is seemingly of no avail. This particular night I was very aggravated because we were not being intimate, she was not reasoning with me, and her pledging had her coming in late hours of the night or very early in the morning. I was waiting up for her because I was really bothered by everything going on and I felt like she owed me a better explanation than what she had given me. After she came in, settled into bed, I made an attempt to be intimate with her. Upon her rejecting me yet again, I responded in a manner that I did not realize existed.

Because I was already at a breaking point, I probably should have left the house or took some other measures to avoid confrontation. Needless to say, I did not. I was not going to be disrespected in my home and in my bed any more than I had already been disrespected. The words she used to express her frustration made me feel so low in that moment. In an instant, I felt like she threw everything she and I had worked for out the window and I reacted. I did not hit her nor did I do anything to intentionally bring her bodily harm. I was, however, physically aggressive enough to bring about an emotional fear. I wanted her to feel how low and humiliated she made me feel. Shortly into the physical altercation my kids were awakened by the noise and screams of me yelling for her to get out of my house. I was yelling at her and pulling on her telling her to get out. During the course of trying to save my marriage, she would frequently say I was asking too much of her to date me and to be intimate with me because it was already a struggle for her to come home every day. If she didn't want to be there, I didn't want her there.

I grew up seeing domestic violence as a common thing in my family and in my community. I heard about my mother having physical altercations with my father and I saw her in many physical altercations with her ex-husband. I grew up vowing that I would never put my hands on a woman in the way I saw them domestically violated. I have always believed any man that has to succumb to physically abusing a woman is the weakest display of a man. Growing up in a single parent home, and having the love and respect for my mother, always gave me the inspiration to be the opposite of what I saw in relationships within my family and in my community.

Yet, I found myself putting on this violent display in front of my kids. In response to my kids screaming and yelling for me to stop, I let her go and immediately starting crying. It was over. Everything I worked so hard to build, was over. I instantly knew my marriage was over. My integrity was shot. My witness was gone. And most of all, my kids were probably scarred for life. I was so outdone. Not only was I angry and disappointed with myself, I was so disappointed with God. I felt like God let me down. All the fasting and praying I had done should have shielded us from something as catastrophic as this. Allow me to share something with you that was very profound, something that made me even more disappointed with God.

As far back as a child as I can remember, my mom has always been very spiritual and intuitive. She has always had what someone would consider a sixth sense. Before the physical altercation, I had been fasting and praying seeking God to restore my marriage. I was only a day or two away from completing my twenty-one day fast when my mother came to me out of the clear blue sky, and asked me if everything was alright between my wife and I. As I shared earlier, I was shielding everyone from the turmoil my marriage was going through. My mother could sense something was wrong but she didn't know the depth of what was going on. After asking me if everything was alright, she proceeded to tell me she had a vision that I hit my wife. She told me to be mindful and not to allow the stress of life to push me to do something like that. I remember replying to my mother that the situation was not that bad. Little did I know that my environment would shift so drastically. Knowing that physical violence is not my character, having my mother share her vision concerning an altercation, coupled with me fasting and praying, I thought surely was enough to keep me from going over the edge.

I don't fully understand why God didn't intervene in the manner in which I felt He should have. I don't know why He allowed me to get that angry. I don't know why He allowed us to fight. I don't know why He didn't give me more strength to resist the urge to become physical with my wife. I may never have a big picture understanding of that dreadful night. There is one thing I do understand. That incident opened my eyes to a hidden and suppressed demon. I never thought it was in me to be that physically aggressive with a woman regardless of how mad I became. Even though God did not remove me from the situation totally, I believe the prayers, fasting, and my mother's vision were all seeds planted to keep me from going further than I did.

If I can encourage anyone who is growing up experiencing domestic violence or you have experienced domestic violence in anyway, I would advise you not to suppress what you have experienced, address it. If you are like me, you are probably asking yourself, how do you address something when you're not aware of its subtle existence? I am glad you asked. If you have been exposed to domestic violence in any way, it is worth taking that situation to God. Ask Him to heal you from wounds you may not even know you have. God knows you better than you will ever know yourself, and the Holy Spirit exposes the deep hidden things within us.

But it was to us that God revealed these things by his Spirit. For his Spirit searches out everything and shows us God's deep secrets. No one can know a person's thoughts except that person's own spirit, and no one can know God's thoughts except God's own Spirit.
1Corinthians 2:10-11 NLT

Issues of the heart can operate somewhat like Tuberculosis. Tuberculosis is an infection that can be transmitted through the airways and you can be carrying the infection without any obvious symptoms. Sometimes it is not until you go to the doctor and they perform an under the skin test, that you find out you have been exposed to the infection. God is the Great Physician, and because he knows every strand of hair on our head, sometimes we need to go to him in prayer and ask him to perform an under the skin spirit test to see what issues we have been exposed to.

Search me, O God, and know my heart! Try me and know my thoughts! Psalms 139:23 ESV

FRANK LUKE

CHAPTER 13
IT'S ALL OVER

All hope for restoring my marriage was lost. Everyone's spirit is disrupted. My wife was in the restroom crying her eyes out, and my beautiful kids were disturbed to the core. Here I was, broken beyond despair. I accepted the harsh reality that my marriage was over. My spirit is crying out to God. Why? What about my kids? What about our ministry? These were just a few of the questions that would race through my mind. I could not understand why God would allow something like this to happen to me; especially with everything I was already enduring for the sake of my family.

I called some close friends that are also ministers and asked them to come over immediately. It was the worst experience ever. I saw the distress on my kids' faces and all I could think about were the many times I felt that same way as a kid when I saw my mother in domestically violent situations. I remembered the horrific feelings of helplessness and fear that were paralyzing and because of me my kids were possibly feeling that same way.

What was even more devastating, as we were all trying to gather ourselves to go to school and work my youngest son did something that crushed my heart. We tried to go on with life as normal. Everyone was still clearly distraught from this uncharacteristic display of aggression from me. My son, while putting on his coat and shouldering his book bag walked over to the fireplace, placed his hand on the picture of his mom and I, bowed his head, and prayed. I wanted to die! My mini me, my cool boy, my twin, is feeling the same pain I felt as a kid if not worse. And I had caused it.

At that moment, I literally wanted to die. I felt like such a failure that I wanted to kill myself for letting my family down. I knew in my heart that suicide was not an option. I cannot lie, I felt like dying but I knew God had more for me to do, and I knew my family needed me. Instead of dying physically or asking God to take me home I decided to die to that insufficient little boy that was still taking up residence within me. I asked God to restore me, reprove me, and renew in me a right spirit. I vowed that I would do everything necessary to address my proclivities and restore my family.

Create in me a clean heart, O God, and renew a steadfast spirit within me. Psalm51:10 NKJV

After our friends brought a little calm back into the house and the dust began to settle, I could see destruction was on the way. My wife's eyes were filled with nothing but anger and disconnect. I went from trying to comfort a woman who was clearly broken as a result of my actions, to a man praying that God would grant me the strength and wisdom necessary to endure the wrath that was about to come. After the tears dried, the look in her eyes was more vengeful than I had ever seen. At that moment, I believed she was going to do what she wanted to do no matter the cost. That night would set the stage for all hell to break loose and for God to show his glory like never before.

Of course, my wife told me it was definitely over and she wasn't looking back. I realized how terrible that night was and I made no excuses for it, but I believed our marriage was bigger than this problem. I refused to believe God couldn't restore our relationship. I knew it was a terrible act but I also knew this act was outside of my character. None of that mattered. She was out: mentally, spiritually, and physically. Because the hurt, anger and intensity was so strong, I eventually moved out of the bedroom to the downstairs bedroom. She was determined even more to get out of the marriage though I was still believing God to save my marriage. What was once a home full of joy, family, life, and friends, was now dark, empty and lonely. We were separated living in the same home and yet we still went to church together and did things with the kids together all in an effort to make things as normal as possible, primarily for the kids. That was the most miserable time of my life. I could deal with the reality of my marriage not working but I'm not a pretentious guy, it was tormenting for me day in and day out to act as if everything was alright.

It was so frustrating trying to reach her and have her to look at the bigger picture; our marriage, our kids, our ministry. I thought we had a pretty good marriage. It wasn't perfect, but we were working it. I went to counseling for a better understanding of myself and I encouraged her to join me at times. She would not stay in counseling with me and no matter what the counselor or friends would say to curb her desire to do things her own way, it was to no avail. She was determined to be out.

Lawyers were paid to have divorce papers drawn and I would agree to sign them because I knew at this point only God could change her heart. Before filing, we had agreed to get back in counseling and we eventually ceremoniously shredded the papers together. Moments like that were short lived. We would live blissfully for weeks, sometimes months before she would revert right back to the unkind, resolute, woman bent on not wanting the marriage.

The stress of trying to save my marriage, keep my kids out of the midst of the storm, and keep the facade that things were not that bad was breaking me down inside and out. I remember taking my kids to a hockey game one night and after this night, I knew I needed God to rescue me in a major way. My kids were enjoying the game, in particular the fights. It was so funny, because it was a surprise for them, they had no idea where we were going.

My son had not dressed for the occasion, he was wearing shorts and sandals. It was so funny looking at him cheering and screaming when a fight erupted, "My grandmother can hit better than you" at the players all while shivering out of control. I was sitting in my seat trying to keep a good disposition for the sake of my kids, but deep down I was so depressed. Everything on the ice and audience seemed to be moving in slow motion. By then, I had lost about fifteen pounds from stressing. I had been receiving anonymous phone calls on a regular basis, suggesting that my wife had alternate reasons for wanting out of the marriage other than just being disconnected. I was tired, and I was ready to give the marriage and its demise totally over to God. I was ready to let her go and allow her to have whatever it was she wanted. Then God spoke to me clearly.

I will never forget how God spoke to me this day. I was tired and frustrated of her rejecting every good thing I could do for her and there was seemingly no progress in us reconciling our marriage. I had taken a forty day love challenge and that was not working. I had called her one day while she was at work and said to her, "You win. I will fall on the sword." Hoping to hear some sort of remorse, but without hesitation she replied, "Ok." I left home to check into a hotel. I was so defeated.

I checked into a hotel to fast and pray, and seek God for His grace and mercy for the decision I was about to make to divorce my wife and leave my family. In my words, prepare me to "fall on the sword." Prepare me to walk away from a marriage I thought would be forever. God spoke a crystal clear word to me, "Be still and know that I am God." I was both humbled because I knew the voice of God had spoken and I was frustrated because I knew I had to go back into the lion's den and eat my words. I armored up (Ephesians 6:11) and went back into battle. When I returned to tell her I wasn't giving up but I was standing on the promises of God, you would have thought I told her one of her dearest love ones had died.

My kids deserved more and I refused to do to them what I saw growing up as a kid. Regardless of how she responded, there was a peace that came over me that was not explainable. I was still hurt and somewhat concerned about the outcome of our future but I was not in fear at all. I knew whatever the outcome was, good or bad, expected or unexpected, God was in control.

CHAPTER 14
A HIDDEN THREAT EXPOSED

Around April 2012, God's words to me in the hotel would make more sense. But before God's glory would manifest in my marriage, my perspective of life would be rattled beyond anything I could have ever fathomed. 2011 was pure hell for me and my family. Broken and now physically separated from my family, I would learn what trust looked like beyond faith. There is a difference. Faith is believing God for something desired or hoped for. You may be seeking God for a healing, a financial breakthrough, a new home, or a new business. The Bible says by faith great things have happened; by faith, the walls of Jericho came down, the Hebrew children passed though the Red Sea. By faith, blind men were given sight. Faith moves mountains, but trust stands still. Trust is simply standing on the will of God. When Jesus was in the garden of Gethsemane He prayed that God would take the cup of crucifixion away from Him. But He transitioned from seeking to trusting. Jesus trusted God's will over His own will. While holding on to faith, and believing God to save my marriage, it wouldn't be long before I would have to trust God's sovereign will.

The stress of trying to save my marriage, keep my kids, family and friends shielded from the truth that my marriage was in shambles, was taking a toll on me. I didn't realize that I had lost a noticeable amount of weight until I went to church one Sunday. I knew I was losing weight, because every time I was around someone that hadn't seen me in a while, that was the first thing they would comment on. The constant reminder was challenging my self-esteem. Insecurity wasn't something that affected me significantly, but I would be lying if I said it wasn't a battle to feel valuable in my own eyes.

It really hit one Sunday morning in church. Service was over, and as usual we were making our rounds meeting and greeting everyone. A female friend of mine walked up to me, greeted me with love, and without hesitation she said, "Frank, you're losing weight. That coat is too big for you!" I immediately knew she didn't mean any harm, because she was clueless as to how volatile things were at the home front. But that didn't help me feel any better knowing that I was an open spectacle.

The tension was not only causing me to lose weight, it was also causing other medical issues to arise. Issues that would expose a hidden threat. I was having an unusual amount of plasma pass from my rectal area after using the restroom. Past years of minor hemorrhoids would occasionally produce a small discharge, but nothing major.

This was major. Every day I was passing large amounts of plasma whether I was using the restroom or not. I knew I needed to see a doctor, but at this point I was scared of what a doctor may say. One day while in the restroom, my wife came in and saw the level of discharge and immediately demanded I go to the doctor.

Deciding not to be a fool any longer, I made the appointment and went to the doctor. After going through the generic procedures of a doctor's visit, she recommended I get a colonoscopy. I was only thirty seven years old at the time, so I was thinking they were just trying to get some more money, or simply experimenting with me. Surely, I was too fit and too young for a colonoscopy. Prepping myself to be violated beyond reason, I made the appointment. The dreaded day arrived. I went to the treatment center and honestly the only thing I was concerned about at that point was whether or not I would be awake for the procedure. Needless to say, I didn't want any part of this. They prepped me, took me to the back, put me to sleep and the rest is history.

FRANK LUKE

CHAPTER 15
THE STARTLING NEWS

All I remember is waking up to my doctor talking as if everything was over. He went on to say they found the cause of the profuse discharge of plasma. It was the result of a level four Fischer tear in my rectum. He asked if I had been straining a lot or had I been in distress? Some friends suggested it was possible stress or strain that could have aided the tear. It was the information that would come a week later that broke me. He went on to say during the procedure they found three polyps within me. He was very disarming, suggesting there was no threat. Granted, polyps are common and with my age and health he was not concerned. He said because of protocol he would send them off to be tested, but for me not to worry.

The following week came, the doctor's office called and said I needed to come in right away for the results. I immediately thought to myself, this cannot be good. We didn't hesitate. We jumped in the car and headed straight over to the doctor's office. Upon walking into the exam room, the doctor announced, "Houston, we have a problem." Ok, that's not what he said, but that's what it sounded like. He said the test results were back and two of the three polyps were benign and one was pre-cancerous.

I couldn't believe it. How could a pre-cancerous cell be growing in me, now of all times? As if my life wasn't already stressful enough. I was devastated. I went through all the mental rants we tend to go through when we feel as if we've been slighted. I eat right. I exercise. I live fairly decent. I love the Lord. Why me? When we feel entitled, we don't realize how much life becomes about us and not about God. Personal pronouns begin to rule as opposed to sacrificial praise.

I was broken. I didn't feel like it was fair. I felt like I didn't deserve this. And I was clueless as to what God was doing with all of this and why. But after sulking a while I began to come to my senses. I was so aggravated, I overlooked the fact the polyps were found before any harm was done. I began to realize, if it wasn't for the stress, if it wasn't for the profuse flow of plasma from a non-related issue, this disease could have and probably would have grown out of control.

God is no respecter of persons. His divine plan for life is far beyond our finite reasoning and love for us is well pass our understanding. The Bible says He will use the foolish things to confound the wise. It didn't make much sense to me why this disease was silently lurking within my body in the first place. I now embrace the necessity of this ordeal because it has enlightened me all the more to how awesome and Sovereign our God is. It has also given me a testimony to share with the world about how good God is.

Surely goodness and mercy shall follow me All the days of my life;
And I will dwell in the house of the Lord Forever.
Psalms 23:6 NKJV

FRANK LUKE

CHAPTER 16
I THOUGHT THIS WOULD
CHANGE THINGS

I thought for sure this experience would give my wife a change of heart, seeing how vulnerable and broken I was and how much turmoil we had gone through. I knew there was no way possible she could stay on this path seeing the level of detriment to our family. I was wrong. Sometimes we don't receive the things we are believing God for, but that doesn't mean He is not God. It can mean it's not time or maybe not His will. We must trust God even when what we are believing Him for doesn't come to pass. I held on to the words of God found in Jeremiah.

Blessed is the man who trusts is in the Lord,
and whose hope is the Lord. Jeremiah 17:7 NKJV

She was not turning back. She made sure my prescriptions were filled, and my immediate needs were met. Outside of that, she had absolutely nothing else to offer. I gave her space to do whatever she felt she needed to do, but I kept my ring on as a reminder that I was trusting God. Later on, she would begin to initiate conversations with me suggesting a possible reconciliation. She said the time apart was therapeutic for her and it gave her an opportunity to think and get herself together.

Among the many discussions with her pertaining to her and the kids returning home, deep down I felt there were some things that were still going unaddressed. There were still the numerous, anonymous, and harassing phone calls I had been receiving. Deep down I still felt like she was not being honest with me concerning her actions and her feelings for me. We were in the driveway of the home we once shared together discussing our plan of reconciliation. Even though I was apprehensive of the unknown I was extremely excited. All I could think about was winning. Winning my family back. The enemy tried to destroy us but God would get the glory. Then it happened.

While we were standing there another harassing phone call came through my phone from an anonymous person suggesting that my wife was not being honest with me. I let her hear the message and like always she denied there was any truth to the message and she did not recognize the voice. I could tell she was caught off guard by what she heard. I strongly suggested to her this was the time to be totally transparent. Too many lies had already played a part in the demise of our marriage, we didn't need to start over like this. I also shared with her a vision I had concerning her unforeseen actions. It was then my heart dropped.

She confessed to everything that I had been thinking and hearing. It was devastating. The roles were immediately shifted, from that dreadful night in March 2011 where I was consoling her because of my actions, now she was trying to give me some solace because of her transgression. While I was grieving the devastating news that had been thrown in my lap I heard in a still small voice ask, "Now that you know, what are you going to do?"

God loves us all. His Word has declared that all things done in the dark will come to the light. I realized God told me to be still not only so she could see the love of God in and through me, but it was so I could know the truth and make a decision based on truth and not emotions alone. In spite of the devastating information that was laid before me, I believed in our marriage. I asked her if she really wanted this marriage, and she said yes. I decided to accept responsibility in what I could have done to contribute to her feeling that there was a need for her to go as far as she did. I forgave her and along with my hurt, I was excited that we had a real opportunity to start afresh. We were so low, I thought with God on our side we couldn't help but go higher.

FRANK LUKE

CHAPTER 17
NOT AGAIN

There is no doubt in my mind God uses absolutely any and everything for the good of those that love Him and are called according to His purpose. If we trust God, the very thing the enemy uses for our bad God will use it for our good. But the operative word is trust. Life can throw some obstacles at you that will truly blindside you and disrupt your course of life. God can and will use whatever challenge or deficiency you're facing to thrust you to a higher calling in Him. But if you refuse to trust the process, you will definitely hinder your progress.

We were definitely on an emotional roller coaster. We were in counseling together and that roller coaster was seemingly going upwards. In spite of the transgressions of our marriage, I believed I finally had the wife I thought I married in 1999. Her brokenness made her a lot humbler and empathetic. I didn't want her to be broken but all I ever wanted from her was to be more compassionate and appreciative of who she had in a husband. I thought all she wanted from me was to be more responsible and supportive. We both had what we were longing for in each other and it was great. Conversations were good, intimacy was good. Not just in the bedroom but in how we considered one another. Most of all, our kids were super happy. Then, out of nowhere it happened again.

About four months into our renewed relationship, she had moved back home, we were attending counseling and after a heated discussion, she again told me she did not want the marriage. She told me she thought she did but it just was not in her to make it work. She went on to say she came back home, because she thought it was the right thing to do and she also thought God would give her the natural affection she so needed and desired to have for me, but He didn't. It was as if she had never confessed, apologized, or even asked for my forgiveness. It was like a light switch was turned off and she was back to where she was before the reconciliation; cold, disconnected, and determined to do what she wanted to do. I felt like a deer caught in the head lights. I was too confused to be devastated but I couldn't help but be concerned for our kids. Once again, I would plead with her not to do this, but she was adamant that she didn't have it in her to love me as a wife should.

This time I didn't put up much of a fight because it was clear to me she wasn't willing to trust God in the restoration process. We filed for divorce again and she moved out again. I was not ready to give up on us, and to be honest, I was scared that she was setting us up for destruction. I, too, had trust issues. We picked up the facade again until the divorce was final. In December 2012, it finally happened. Many times in the past, she would file for divorce and take it back, primarily because deep down in her heart she knew we had a blessed marriage and God's favor was on our life.

I was participating in an outreach program with my kids when I received a baffling phone call from my wife. She engaged me with pleasant small talk and she was trying to come participate in the outreach with us. This was strange because just two or three days prior, she was very adamant in not wanting to reconcile. We would meet later on that night to converse about us and where we were going with our lives. It was then that she told me the divorce was final. I thought it would be no big deal but that's not so. As a child of God, we understand His words are not just manuscripts we read and casually walk away from. His word is the very essence of our spiritual, social, and emotional awareness to good and bad, right or wrong. In His Word He says what He has joined together let no man come between. I felt His disappointment as well as my own. I had to suck it up and move forward.

I really don't know what the lesson was to come out of our divorce. I do know, it showed me life happens and all you and I can do is respond to the voice of God to the best of our ability. I'm sure if Jacob knew his uncle Laban was going to deceive him and not honor his word when he told him he could have his daughter Rachel if he worked for him for seven years, he would have approached the situation a lot differently. However, Laban tricked him into marrying his oldest daughter Leah and told him if he wanted Rachel he had to work for him another seven years. Jacob probably went through many of the same emotional thought patterns we would have gone through. I'm not working another seven years, It's not worth it. Seeing that Jacobs name meant trickster, he may have contemplated how he could outwit Laban. But instead, he accepted his reality and pursued his passion, and eventually received his reward.

We must understand that God is sovereign and this is why He sent His Son to die for our sins. Nothing catches God off guard and in Him there is a sufficient grace and an abundance of mercy. We won't understand everything that happens in our life but we are held responsible to trust God even when we don't understand. I am reminded of a quote I hold close to my heart by Dr. Charles Stanley who said, "Obey God and leave the consequences to Him."

CHAPTER 18
ONE LAST TRY

After accepting the harsh reality that my marriage was legally over, and after many years of living as a family man I was now thrusted into being a single man. It may sound good to some, the thought of being single after so many years of living for one person. For me, it was a deflating reality. I never imagined that living for God and striving to do the best I could do, would be so disappointing. By no means am I trying to portray the role of someone that was perfect in marriage. I know there were many times I disappointed my wife emotionally by neglecting my responsibility of being the leader God anointed me to be financially. I know I've said some things, and I've done some things that I wasn't proud of. But all in all, I was committed to doing God's will and growing through my inadequacies. In spite of the issues that come with marriage, we had a blessed union.

It took me some time to comprehend why God would allow something that was so beautiful, such a blessing to so many people come to an end. And it hit me; He is God. He reserves the right to allow, to not allow, or to do what it is He chooses to do according to His will. God doesn't sit back and slap His knee when things are disrupting and blowing up in our face. No. God wants nothing but the best for us. The Bible says that "We have not a God who can't be reached with the affections of our infirmities but was in all points tempted as we are, without sin (Hebrews 4:15). God feels our pain. This is why He sent His son. Not only does He relate to our pain, but He helps us overcome. Being free moral agents, God will not impose Himself on you, that's His sovereign right. Instead we have the liberty to make choices that honor God or dishonor God. Everything else in between is part of the process.

I began to embrace my newfound journey and the process of redefining myself. I can't lie, that process was full of rewards and disappointments. There were days I was excited because I was managing my life pretty well on my own which was somewhat new for me. I am the kind of guy that works hard and brings the money home for my wife to manage and make sure all the bills were taken care of. She enjoyed managing the household, being an administrator is one of her major gifts. Now, doing it myself was a rewarding accomplishment. I didn't do it as fluently as she did it. I had to set reminders in my phone for everything; mortgage, cable, cell phone, gas, electric, grocery shopping, laundry, etc. I never knew running out of toilet paper in an untimely manner could be so heart breaking. My ex-wife handled all those things so effortlessly. The things that came naturally for her were work for me. But I was working it. It was in those times that I would have mental setbacks. That's when I started to play the blame game.. The only way I could continuously feel good about my situation when things would get challenging, I had to blame her for our demise.

But through counseling, good friends and confidants, I received some of the best advice I could have received. I was out with my real-estate agent looking for a home. Noticing I was in somewhat of a slump, she advised me, "Luke, Stop fighting it. If you're hurting, its ok. If you're feeling good, its ok. It is a part of the process and the more you try to fight it the more you prolong the progress." Her words were so liberating. Sometimes it's the small nuggets that form the stone.

I learned to accept everyday as it came and to take one day at a time. Like Jacob, I didn't receive the promise of my labor immediately, and I felt my reward was unfair. Outside of my immediate feelings, I knew I would receive God's promises according to the purpose He has for my life.

Months went by, adjustments were constantly being made, I was getting acclimated with the single life and learning to co-parent with my ex-wife was not a challenge. Granted, compared to what we've seen in divorces that were bitter and the kids were caught in the middle of an ugly contention, we were very cordial and accommodating. During this time, she would periodically suggest that she wanted to entertain us reconciling yet again. I thought it was the craziest thing. Not just her wanting to reconcile again in spite of all that had transpired, but the fact that I was entertaining it.

This was one of the more confusing times for me. On one hand, I was moving on and excited about my future and all that God had in store for me. On the other hand, she was so convincing and I was still missing the family unit we once had. There was a void that at times seemed like it could never be fulfilled without that which was so familiar. I was heartbroken, confused, angry, and struggling with trusting my heart with her all over again. I was in my living room toiling with the question. Do I give this a chance again or do I trust God with another plan? I spoke with God and I asked Him if it was His will for us to reconcile. I remember reasoning with God and I said to Him, there were three things I needed her to take a definitive stance on. If she was willing to honor these three things I was requesting of her that day, that would be my sign God desired for us to reconcile. If she didn't, that would be the sign that God was pleased with me moving on with my life. Feeling a very soothing peace of God and meditating on the words of wisdom from my counselor, I was ready to take a chance once again. My counselor's words of wisdom were a constant ringing in my ear. In one of my personal sessions, he said I would be blessed either way. If I chose to stay with or now stand without her, he said there will be consequences with either choice, but I will be blessed. I arose from my living room sofa with much confidence and peace that God heard my cry and He would honor my request.

Now to some theologians this may sound far-fetched. God does not reason with man. I beg to differ. The God we serve is full of grace, mercy and love. In the book of Isaiah, He said to the children of Israel, "Come let us reason together." Jesus said that His sheep shall know My voice. It is God's will for us to live out our godly marriages in honor of Him. However, divorce is an act of man's selfishness and rebellion against God's will. When that choice is made, this is where His grace abounds. The spouse that has been rejected does not have to dwell in bondage. By no means am I suggesting that anyone should take advantage of His grace. Paul addresses this compromise.

What then? Shall we sin because we are not under law
but under grace? Certainly not! Romans 6:15NKJV

Please understand, though you're not called to live in bondage there are consequences that come with every decision. God hates divorce, and regardless of who's at fault, there will be consequences that come with dishonoring God's plans. Thank God, trouble don't last always.

I trusted the word and will of God to save my marriage, it was not my desire for us to divorce. I believed that I was both released by way of the state of Georgia and the biblical law of grace, and yet I was open to respond to God's will of unconditional love, and restorative plan for my family. She pulled up at the house, I took a deep breath and said to myself in the words of my daughter, "Let's do this man." All I was standing on was the confidence of God. I had so many doubts that she was going to agree to all three of my request. One request in particular. Setting myself up for yet another heart breaking disappointment just didn't make sense. When you're living for God, many times you will have to make decisions that don't make sense to you. The Word of God says that He will take the foolish things to confound the wise.

I had prepared my questions carefully and postured my heart for the potential casualty. To my surprise, when I asked her the first question without hesitation she agreed. Wow! I was thinking this might be good. The next question was the same. Without any hesitation, she agreed to my second request. Now the drum rolls in my ear and the butterflies in my stomach have begun. The big question is at hand. This question would determine how serious and genuine she was about us reconciling and doing the work that was necessary to assure me she was in it to win it. I asked the final, deal making or deal breaking question. And just like the other two questions, she responded with much confidence and without hesitation. Her words to me were mind boggling. She said, "Oh no, I'm not going to be able to do that."

I could not believe it. I let her suck me in again just to be let down all over again. I told her I was done. I was offended and I could not believe, the one thing that meant the most to me she was not willing to do it. It wasn't anything unreasonable. As a matter of fact, with everything we had been through these last couple of years, I thought it was very reasonable. If you're wondering why I'm not revealing the questions, it's not because they were inappropriate. They were personal. This book is meant to inspire, uplift and reveal the power of God's infinite wisdom and plan for your healing.

That was it for me. That was what I needed to move on and I truly believed God was pleased with my decision. Then a monkey wrench was thrown into the equation. Approximately a month had gone by. One Sunday morning we were in church and it was as if God spoke to the pastor and told him we were going to be there. It was as if He told him everything we were going through and then told him to show a video that addressed our circumstances and preach on it. Everything from the video presentation to the message was directly in line with our scenario. We would return to my home, and in my mind this was it. She had just graduated and received her master's degree. I told her that was my last celebratory act with her. I celebrated and honored her for graduating because she deserved it. It was now time to move on, raise our kids, and establish clear boundaries. But before leaving to go home she would pull another rabbit out of the hat. She came in and to my surprise, without hesitation she decided to adhere to the third request that was asked approximately a month ago.

It was a euphoric moment. It's always advantageous to be optimistic when it comes to what God can do. Without hesitation I pushed pass all of my proclivities so that I could give her all the assurance she needed to feel safe and protected. I embraced her, told her I loved her and said to her in the words of my daughter, "Let's do this man."

CHAPTER 19
WAS IT ME? GOD? OR BOTH?

Though she didn't adhere to the third and most important question when I wanted her to, and I was seemingly disregarding the oath I made with God, all I could focus on was my family finally getting back together. This time she really came across as if she was repentant and redeemed. It appeared that God was moving in His own time and not mine. I was willing to embrace that maybe I was off. I mean, I am human. Things began to happen so fast. During the early phases of the relationship when she was checking out emotionally and checking back in emotionally, she would periodically say she wanted to move and she wanted a new wedding ring. She wasn't a person that was hung on material things, she made sure her family had an abundance of the things we desired. So, I was honored to oblige her in that manner. I felt compelled to give her whatever her heart desired, in spite of whatever happened in the past. She deserved it.

I went out and purchased her a three-carat diamond ring to her liking. I decided to re-enact how I proposed to her in 1999. But this time I was determined to do it a little better. When I proposed to her in 1999, she was laying in the bed asleep and I knelt by the bed with roses in one hand and one-and-a-half carat ring in the other. Don't judge me, I was young, that's all I could afford. Feeling my presence beside the bed, she awoke to a dozen roses and an engagement ring staring her in the face.

Fast forward thirteen years later. She didn't know I had purchased the ring. I waited until she went to sleep; I drew a sign that said Will You Marry Me? I placed the sign in the bathroom on the vanity along with the ring. When she awoke in the morning to go to the restroom which was her normal routine, I arose from the bed, kneeled at the door way, and waited for her to come out of the restroom. When I heard her sigh, I knew I had her. She came out, saw me kneeling, and I asked her again would she marry me.

It was awesome. My kids were excited. Life couldn't be better. We had seemingly defied all the odds. Not to mention, shortly afterwards, God didn't just bless us with another home but He blessed us with a brand new home in the very same school district I was trying to move in when I was single. There was no way anyone could tell me that we didn't win and God didn't get the glory. The way things were falling into place only God could orchestrate something like that. Little did I know this dream would be so short lived, again.

We were back. My family was back together and stronger than ever. Seeing the joy on my kids' faces and at times stepping back to see the hand of God on everything was priceless. I would soon learn that at the end of every blessing there is an unforeseen challenge. A few months after moving into our new home and getting everything settled, it wasn't long before I would see and hear subtle things that reminded me of those dark moments in our relationship. I would look past it because that time was very traumatic for everyone and I didn't want to seem as if I was being delusional, thinking everything was supposed to be perfect. Of course it's a process, this is why we were in counseling. I know with everything I'm about to say you're going to think I'm making this stuff up. I'm not.

Four months into our newfound relationship, my wife began to take a negative stance against our union again. It erupted on a day we were leaving counseling. Because I had been hearing and seeing things in her behavior that caused me to be apprehensive, I didn't want to feel that way and I didn't want to hinder our progression. That was my reality and I thought what better place to address it than with our counselor. Big mistake. When I shared with the counselor my concerns and my challenges with trusting some of her current behavior, she hit the roof. She copped a major attitude. I couldn't believe it. I thought this is what we come to counseling for. To discuss the challenges, we have with one another, listen to the advice of our counselor, and practice doing relationships better. It was happening again. She was drifting back into the exact behavior as before.

On our ride home from the counselor's office, I tried to communicate with her to better understand what could have possibly gone wrong. After a few minutes of intense discussion, her words to me in that moment sounded the alarm. Her words and her tone were all too familiar. The actions that were common to follow her disposition were so disrespectful and hurtful I was compelled to pull over onto the side of the road, off of a major freeway. I said to her, at this point in our relationship and with everything we've been through together, if you can fix your mouth to say something like that to me, you can have this marriage. I was done!

I got out of the car and began to walk. As I was walking, the level of disbelief, hurt and the anger was overwhelming. I was furious. I was just as mad at God, again, as I was with her. I wondered why would He encourage me to go back if He knew this would be our demise. No matter how I tried to look at it, it made absolutely no sense. I didn't understand how she could allow that misunderstanding in the counseling office to lead her to forget all that we had overcome. It wasn't that long into the walk before God sent a messenger --my neighbor-- to pull over on the side of the road and say exactly what I needed to hear to know that God had a greater plan for my life. I am a living witness, that God is always speaking. Either were not listening, or we haven't been in communion with God enough to even know what we're listening for. I returned to the car with my mind made up. I was not going to allow my anger or frustration to get the best of me nor was I going to accept anything less than what I felt I deserved from my wife. If she was content with her actions, I was content with trusting that still small voice in it all. A couple of months went by with no progression in our storybook reconciliation. The decline was more and more every day. A day after celebrating her birthday, she asked me yet again to go with her to file for divorce. Unbelievable!

Without any regrets nor with any hesitation, I willfully obliged her and signed the divorce papers for my final time. I decided to move out for a few reasons. One, I knew God blessed us with this home for a reason if it was only for her and the kids to have a better home and school environment. Two, I wasn't going to bring anymore disturbance to that environment than was already there. Three, the environment was just too hostile and I didn't feel the peace of God this time around as I did before. Last but not least, I believed if there would be any salvaging of our marriage this time, I needed to be out of the home.

At my lowest position in life, I found God in the best way. Not only did I decide to leave the home we had just purchased, I also removed myself from any entitlement of our other property. Whether this was the right or wrong decision to make at the time, I'm not sure. What I was sure of, it was time for me to get myself together. I got off of my soap box and went to work. It was time for me to be about my Father's business. The only way I could do it was to trust God with everything. I was at my lowest. No home of my own, finances were at an all-time low, and the credit score I had so proudly built up over the years diminished because of poor decisions I had made.

CHAPTER 20
THE BLESSING IN IT ALL

Here's the blessing in it all. Now I need you to put your spiritual thinking caps on so you can see how God uses everything for the good to them that love Him and, so you can see His sovereign and infinite wisdom. Divorce papers have been filed, I've moved out of our new home, our kids are devastated and confused yet again, and I am baffled as to why this is happening again. I toiled with the Lord and I asked how He could have allowed this to happen to us again? What did I do wrong? And then it hit me.

God knows everything imaginable and unimaginable about us. From the moment we're born to the to the time of our departure, we are all on a journey that is orchestrated by decisions, questions, answers, trials, ups and downs and errors that all lead us to our ultimate destination. There are happy times and sad times. There are good times and bad times. There are highs and lows, peaks and valleys all in an effort to direct us to God's righteousness and draw us closer to God's plans for our life.

In this timeline of experiences, God wants us to learn of Him by way of His Word, prayer, and through the endurance of life's trials. He is the only One that has infinite wisdom. Some of our decisions will not be well-advised, some of our decisions will. Some of our decisions will be faith-based and spirit led, and some of our decisions will not be so spirit led. At the end of it all, we must trust that the manifestation of our spirit led decisions rest in God's will and plan for our life. There is an argument called the Teleological argument. This argument suggests that the design of the universe and its function has an intelligent design and purpose which implies there must be an intelligent and purposeful God who created it. No decision good or bad, right or wrong is wasted in God's plan. There is not one experience unforeseen by the Almighty. It is our responsibility to learn from every encounter of our past. Grow from every mistake of today, and trust in Him for a better tomorrow. The infinite knowledge and wisdom of God doesn't give our finite beings a pass to do what we want to do, as the Bible lets us know, we get what we put out.

Do not be deceived: God cannot be mocked. A man reaps what he sows. Whoever sows to please their flesh, from the flesh will reap destruction; whoever sows to please the Spirit, from the Spirit will reap eternal life. Galatians 6:7,8 NIV

It wasn't until the divorce was final and months of seeking God had gone by that I would better understand why I was here, challenged in a way that I had not been challenged in all the days of my adult Christian life. I shared with you earlier the conversation I had with God on my living room sofa concerning the three questions I needed my wife to answer in order for me to seriously consider reconciliation. I knew He heard and received my request. Also, remember I shared with you the wisdom my counselor imparted into me; he said based on the circumstances and the desire in my heart to please God, if I chose to return home to be with my family I would be blessed. And if I chose to accept the reality of divorce and all the disappointments that came with it and move on with my life as a single man, I would be blessed. He also said, in spite of being blessed there would be consequences with either decision.

God knowing all things allowed her to adamantly refuse to respond to the third and most important request for us to reconcile. It was up to me to honor the words I had spoken to God. When we attended church service that mother's day weekend, weeks after she refused to answer my third question, it was very apparent the message was speaking directly to our marital demise.

Today, I don't believe that message was for me, I believe it was intended for her. I was very clear on wanting my marriage and wanting to reconcile before the divorce manifested. After the divorce, there were major trust issues and though she was really trying to convince me she was willing to do what was necessary for us to be together as a family, when she refused to respond to this simple question, I knew then she wasn't as committed as she was presenting herself to be. God gave me peace to move forward as a single man and co-parent our children as single parents. However, the element of our humanity called fear was still influencing me. Fear of what would happen to my kids if I wasn't there. Fear of what would happen to her if I let go of the dream of our thirteen-year relationship in ministry and family. Fear of ever obtaining the experience of being happily married, enjoying the days of coming home to a wife and kids. My fear provoked me to doubt God. I disregarded the conversation He and I had all in the name of wanting my family back.

CHAPTER 21
THANK GOD FOR
GRACE AND MERCY

God knowing everything imaginable and unimaginable about me knew I would respond out of my insecurities, therefore, He made provision. His will for my life would come to pass, but not before I would remarry my wife and divorce again. I accepted her appeal for us to reconcile and I believed her when she said she was willing to commit to doing God's will. Her words and many of her actions were very convincing, however, God knew the deeper issues of the heart. And it wouldn't be long before the issues of her heart would manifest yet again. God knew the hidden things that rested deep within, things my finite being couldn't comprehend. But before everything would hit the fan, we would be blessed with everything we had been praying for. The new home we purchased, was a home I wanted to purchase while I was single in the very same neighbor I desired to move in. Before we divorced, she would always speak that she wanted a new home, and we had it. She would also speak that she wanted a new wedding ring. She would receive that, all three carats of it. It was surreal how everything was coming together. The kids were in a great school district, our neighbors were great, the stage was set for a story book ending. But since He knew I would adhere to the desire to bring my family back together, He blessed us tremendously with the desires of our heart. Wanting my family back together was a noble thing. I have learned, regardless of how noble a thing is, God's will, supersedes nobility. I realize now, through grace and mercy she has obtained many of the tangible things she was desiring and my kids are in the community I was desiring. As for me, the financial woes and the discomforts I have had to endure were a direct result of my initial disobedience. I am not crying over spilled milk or having a hum drummed pity party. If it had not been for the rise and fall of our relationship, I'm not sure when I would have responded to the call of God on my life to preach the acceptable year of the Lord.

The Spirit of the Lord is upon me, because he hath anointed me to preach the gospel to the poor; he hath sent me to heal the brokenhearted, to preach deliverance to the captives, and recovering of sight to the blind, to set at liberty them that are bruised, To preach the acceptable year of the Lord. And he closed the book, and he gave it again to the minister, and sat down. Luke 4:18 KJV

My relationship with God has grown tremendously because of my story. I used to believe I knew God and I had a very sound relationship with Him, but now I am intimately connected with God in a way that is unprecedented. I have spent time with Him both in the wilderness and in the garden. My trials have taught me that the love of God works better than any pain reliever on the market. There is no pain that He can't heal. This topic has been with me for over eight years.

My journey has been to me like a cocoon is to a caterpillar. There were many times I felt trapped in confusion, mediocrity and doubt. But I've always believed there was more that God wanted out of me. Timing is everything to God. Just like that caterpillar has to stay in that cocoon until its transformation on the inside is fulfilled. God will allow you to go through some challenging things because He knows there is something greater in you that has to be developed from the inside out. When that time comes, it's mind blowing to see what God will do in and through your life when you trust the process. When you look at the story of Joseph, he went from being his father's *favorite*, his brothers *fallen* victim, to second in command to pharaohs *fortune*. He journeyed from *favor, fallen,* to *fortune* all in God's timing.

My ex-wife and I are good friends and we co-parent our children extremely well. My testimony serves notice to the world that you don't have to be disgruntled and bitter with your ex-spouse. When it's all said and done, if you are a child of God you are required to forgive and love through it all. Despite all of our differences she and I are both determined to not lay our childhood burdens nor the demise of our marriage at our children's feet.

The most valuable lesson I've learned throughout my entire journey is that God doesn't make mistakes. In spite of it all, when you trust in Him there is no way but up. Every chemical imbalance, every death, and every challenge in my life that has not broken me has built me for this life of abundance right now. It would have been beautiful for us to have that storybook ending relationship. It will be even more beautiful, knowing my testimony along with the inspiration of the Holy scriptures can and will help you have that storybook ending. Honor God and trust Him with your life and you will see; life is not all good, it's all God.

ABOUT THE AUTHOR

Frank Luke is the founder of Frank Luke Ministries. He brings more than fifteen years of Christian service to the body of Christ. Twelve of those years he served as an associate minister at New Life Church in Decatur, GA under his Senior Pastor, Marlin Harris.

He is an ordained reverend, and he has obtained certificates in Christian counseling and Contemporary Theology.

With a passion to see men, young and old evolve and thrive in purpose, and live out their God ordained destiny, Frank Luke established Men Leading From Their Knees Men's ministry.

Frank Luke resides in Atlanta, GA. with his three kids, Aric Flemming Jr., Nia and Zion Luke.

Visit www.franklukeministries.com

Made in the USA
Lexington, KY
08 July 2017